Order this book online at www.trafford.com
or email orders@trafford.com

Most Trafford titles are also available at major online book retailers.

Note for Librarians: A cataloguing record for this book is available from Library
and Archives Canada at www.collectionscanada.ca/amicus/index-e.html

Printed in Victoria, BC, Canada.

ISBN: 978-1-4251-8167-3 (soft)
ISBN: 978-1-4251-8168-0 (ebook)

*Our mission is to efficiently provide the world's finest, most comprehensive book publishing
service, enabling every author to experience success. To find out how to publish your book, your
way, and have it available worldwide, visit us online at www.trafford.com*

Trafford rev. 11/24/2009

 www.trafford.com

North America & international
toll-free: 1 888 232 4444 (USA & Canada)
phone: 250 383 6864 ♦ fax: 812 355 4082

Lillie Dillie Start Wealthy

Early Wealth Management for Kids

Written by

Leanoria R. Johnson

MultiplicationShake.com

Woodbury, Minnesota

www.MultiplicationShake.com

Lillie Dillie Start Wealthy

Early Wealth Management for Kids

DVDs, Music CDs and workbooks mentioned in this book are sold separately. There is no reason you should not order today. Visit wwwMultiplicationShake.com, www.GroomToBeWealthy.com or e-mail orders@MultiplicationShake.com for our music, media products and workbook information. Our Groom To Be Wealthy Project is a workbook that contains the how-to's of budgeting, calculating compound interest, the rule of 72 and many more hands-on experiences.

Websites mentioned in this book are for educational use only. All websites contained herein are copyright and property of their respective and property of their owners. Other applicable federal and state laws may also protect the web sites that are listed, mentioned, and reviewed in this book. MultiplicationShake.com and Leanoria R. Johnson have no responsibility and assumes no liability of any nature for the content of any websites that is in this book. The content of these websites may change. The content of this book is priceless. Many valuable lessons are throughout this book.

Every effort has been made to give copyright holders credit, and we apologize in advance for any omissions. We would be pleased to insert the appropriated acknowledgements in any subsequent edition of this publication.

Library of Congress ISBN: 978-14251-8167-3

TABLE OF CONTENTS

About the Author

Leanoria R. Johnson, an award-winning teacher, wrote <u>Lillie Dillie Start Wealthy:</u> <u>Early Wealth Management for Kids </u>to inspire kids and young adults to learn early how to manage their money. She has provided a relevant teaching tool on a level and in a language that the potential life-long managers can understand. Their early awareness and application of concepts such as budgeting, compound interest and the rule of 72, will hopefully lead them to "wealth". Leanoria wrote Lillie Dillie Start Wealthy to provide parents, grandparents, teachers, and other leaders a priceless teaching aid! Our educational resource integrates literacy, practical money management strategies, practice sheets, and many other valuable lessons all in one book. It fills in the gap of financial education. It is a great source to use at home and in school with your current literacy and math curriculum.

Educator, author, Leanoria R. Johnson, rules for EARLY money management practices taught in her book, <u>Lillie Dillie Start Wealthy: Early Wealth Management</u> <u>for Kids.</u> She has created classic information which will be used weekly by some readers and very often by others to facilitate family and group discussions. The Teaching Aids section provides all readers with more relevant materials that engage the learners in impacting hands on experiences in budgeting and setting goals, too. The Teaching Aids section also provides schedules, enrichment activities relating to money management, reading, math, and arts and crafts. She created songs that teach concepts about money and math. Her Math music CD provides vocals and instrumental music to inspire the children to be happy learners. She knows the power of getting the children moving, dancing, singing, color-coding. These are key factors in assisting children in retaining information and improving their achievement. She has a Daily Tracking Practice tool and movie clips on her website to make it easy for you to teach money management and math processes. Leanoria covered many areas because she is a parent and teacher and know what we need. She has a heart for the young and for parents-teachers. As she thought about what a parent and a teacher needs, she created it. Now, all you have to do is appreciate the hard work and do the training at an early age. Now, she invites you to view the links to her awards and accomplishments by visiting her website www.MultiplicationShake.com.

How to Use This Book

Lillie Dillie Start Wealthy: Early Wealth Management for Kids was written to help parents believe that they are the first and best teachers of their children. After reading this book, readers will have a big picture of how to manage money and build wealth over a period of time. This book is easy to read and easy to understand. The intra-comprehension questions support immediate response and analysis of comprehension levels. Parents and teachers find it easy to discuss the context with their students with these questions. Students are grateful to have easy access to their responses to the intra-comprehension questions when asked, "What was the story about?"

All users of this book are strongly encouraged to use our upbeat audio CD, "The Multiplication Shake" to get long lasting results in teaching the basic money management terms that are in the Teaching Aids Section of the book. The tracks with vocals or the instrumental music will work. We recommend teaching a specific set of words as vocabulary and spelling words. After you have introduced the simple meanings that we have provided for you, play musical chairs by placing one or two words in each chair. Choose 5, 8, or 12 players. Have one less chair than players at all times. Play the music and stop the music. The child who is left without a chair, must define the words. Remove that player and remove another chair. All players and students watching are responsible for writing down correct spellings and meanings of the basic money management terms.

Parent's Use of the Book

Use the schedules in the Teaching Aids section of the book to schedule a consistent time that you and your child will read and discuss <u>Lillie Dillie Start Wealthy: Early Wealth Management Book for Kids.</u> Instruct your child to read and write answers to the intra-comprehension questions that are with the contents of the book. Answers may be written in the book's margins. After your child reads, discuss his/her answers to the intra-comprehension questions. Accept sensible answers and correct unethical remarks. Monitor the completion of the activities that are in the Teaching Aids section of the book. The money management, reading, math and art activities will challenge your child to visualize pictures, create mind movies, become creative thinkers and increase their academic and financial management skills. Share your personal experiences where relevant. Thoroughly, review the samples of simple interest, compound interest, and the rule of 72 on page 65 with your child. Visit your local credit union or bank and start saving for the future immediately.

Use the mini projects and hands on budgets and visual boards to direct your child in fulfilling his or her dreams. Also, teach money management skills and set financial goals with your child. Answer keys are available to assist you. Use the resourceful websites within the book to help your child to gain the advantage edge of using technology. Use our instrumental music and songs that teach reading, math, and social studies to increase academic achievement.

Teacher's Use of the Book

Use <u>Lillie Dillie Start Wealthy: Early Wealth Management for Kids</u> adjunct to your district's reading curriculum. Each student will answer the intra-comprehension questions in the margins of the book or on another sheet of paper. Instruct students to reflect on parts of the book that were similar to experiences in their own lives. The book is pictureless intentionally and students will need to visualize daily. They will draw pictures that they visualized as they reflect on what they have read and have completed the reading activities. Use the Teaching Aids section of the book to enrich the learning experience of money management skills with hands on fun and various academic lessons. Use the "Lillie Dillie Come Alive" activities to bring parts of the book to real life. Use the mini projects to teach economic standards and prepare students for life experiences relating to managing money. The educational songs will support long term learning of academic and financial concepts.

Thoroughly, review the samples of simple interest, compound interest, and the rule of 72 on page 65 with your students. Make up more simple problems for them to work. Help them understand how applying the concepts to their lives will benefit their future. Arrange for field trips to a local credit union or bank and encourage your students to start saving for the future immediately.

After School and Enrichment Program Director's Use of the Book

Use <u>Lillie Dillie Start Wealthy: Early Wealth Management for Kids</u> to inspire creative students to create pictures for the text and to create role plays using the text. Our hands-on visual boards and budgets N' crafts activities liven up the day or the end-of-the day! You will find them in the Teaching Aids section of our book. Follow our step-by-step instructions for mini projects and various academic and financial lessons. Lead students into building a solid foundation in money management. Guide them in applying our real life-like money management practices in their lives. They will increase their chances of building wealth in the future. Be a leading force in adding "financial education" as a core value in your program. Take them on field trips to financial institutions.

Your students will also benefit from our hands on **Groom To Be Wealthy Project**. They will learn money management practices that may lead them to becoming above financially secure, wealthy!

Children and Youth Program Coordinators and Ministers' Use of this Book

Use <u>Lillie Dillie Start Wealthy: Early Wealth Management for Kids</u> to enjoy shared reading. Discuss the principles and encourage readers to think of how the concepts in the book relate to their personal lives. Use the various types of budgets in the Teaching Aids section of the book to compare and contrast budgets for kids, teens, and young adults. Use the mini project and hands on visual boards and budgets to instill vital money management principles in students. Our music adds excitement and increases academic interest and achievement. Seeing a budget for fifty cents will inspire youth who make a small salary to budget their paycheck wisely. Your students will also benefit from our hands on **Groom To Be Wealthy Project**. They will learn money management practices that may lead them to becoming above financially secure, wealthy!

Invite the author in to speak and teach about simple interest, compound interest, the rule of 72 and other principles in <u>Lillie Dillie Start Wealthy</u>.

Book Clubs and Self-Motivated Readers' Use of the Book

Each reader will need a copy of the book. Read as you normally do and answer the intra-comprehension questions. Reflect and evaluate the concepts in the book. Apply principles to your life that will help you become excellent money managers. Use the Teaching Aids as interactive exercises to become more responsible money managers who will be excited about tracking money and building wealth. Invite the author to interact with your members.

Reading or Literacy Section

This section contains the story of Lillie Dillie and her daughter Braidee, along with the intra-comprehension questions.

Lillie Dillie's Childhood Years

Lillie Dillie lived down South in a little three-room, wooden white house. Patches of grass struggled to grow in the hard red dirt. Lillie Dillie and her friends had to jump over a wire fence to get the wild plants that they used to cook greens in their pretend play. They dug up plugs of dirt to play mud cakes, too. Lillie Dillie was a joyful little girl who had pony tails that were longer than those of her friends. Lillie Dillie's beautician pressed her hair with hot straightening comb free of charge. The trade off was Lillie Dillie would run errands for her. She was old and her legs were crippled. Lillie Dillie's mother, Ms. Helen, owned a set of black straightening comb irons, too. One Sunday, when Ms. Helen had gone to church, Lillie Dillie took a match and turned on the gas fire on their old white stove. She heated the straightening comb. She greased a front section of her long hair. The hot irons were too hot. Lillie Dillie's long hair scorched and then burned off. It seared in the hot irons. Lillie Dillie became overtaken with fear. She started plotting how to hide the burned off hair before her mom returned home. She thought, "I can pull this long section to the side and MaDear won't be able to tell what happened." Lillie Dillie was forced to wear bangs and continued to wear the front of her hair sideways after the hair grew back.

Lillie Dillie was the baby girl of the family. She had four older brothers and one older sister. Ms. Helen enjoyed cooking banana puddings and sweet potato pies. She had a business mind, too. She owned a home at one point in her life. She owned a restaurant at one point in her life, too. Major life changes affected Ms. Helen's family. She lost her home, her restaurant, and most importantly, her oldest daughter in a car accident and Ms. Helen was seriously injured, too. All of the pain and anguish changed the economic status of the family. The family faced some difficult times. Lillie Dillie was very young when the unfortunate circumstances affected her family. Lillie Dillie could only remember seeing a bloody dress soaking in a tin bucket.

Intra-Comprehensive Questions (ICQ) – What might have been some of the changes that came to the family? Are you grateful for what your family has? Explain.

One could see why Lillie Dillie became so special to the family. She was appreciated because she was alive and the only girl, now. Ms. Helen got well from the accident and this comforted Lillie Dillie. Lillie Dillie was such a lovable little girl because she loved serving elderly people. Everyday Lillie Dillie visited Mrs. Boykin and Mrs. Wilson. She loved running errands for the old ladies. Mrs. Wilson lived in a wooden green house that had a screened-in front porch. She had roosters and chickens clucking all over the yard. Mrs. Wilson would send Lillie Dillie to Lee and Terry Grocery Store with a dollar.

The neighborhood store was about half a mile from the old ladies' houses. Lillie Dillie would arrive after the noon hour, ready to help out in any way that she could. Mrs. Wilson would send Lillie Dillie to buy some fresh vegetables for a delicious soup. She'd tell Lillie Dillie to buy a bag of potatoes for 50 cents, a tomato for 10 cents, and a bag of mixed vegetables for 35 cents. Lillie Dillie would proudly hand Mr. Terry the $1.00.

Mr. Terry would not give Lillie Dillie her change until they had sung their change game. The song was as follows:

> Lillie Dillie came to my store. Lillie Dillie bought three things once more. Lillie Dillie, tell me how much change do you get back from a dollar?

Lillie Dillie would happily sing her part:

> I know the answer. I know the answer. That's so easy. All I have to do is subtract 95 cents from a dollar.

Intra-Comprehensive Questions (ICQ): How much did Lillie Dillie spend in all? How much change will Lillie Dillie get back?

Lillie Dillie was very honest. She was taught that honesty is the only policy. She would get in big trouble, if she told Mrs. Wilson half of the truth. Lillie Dillie took Mrs. Wilson all of her change. She never thought about lying and saying that she lost the change in the gravel street. When Lillie Dillie was just about to close the screen door, Mrs. Wilson would say, "Lillie Dillie, thank you Darling for going to the store for me. I want to bless you with a quarter or twenty-five cents." And Lillie Dillie would say, "Thank you. You are welcome. I'll be back to see about you." Lillie Dillie stuffed her quarter under her heels in her white bow tie tennis shoes.

The following day arrived and it was Lillie Dillie's day to go to the store for Mrs. Boykin. Mrs. Boykin would give Lillie Dillie $2.00 for fruits and juices for fruit smoothies and cinnamon for tea cakes. Mrs. Boykin sent Lillie Dillie to the Cooper Road Market for fresh vegetables. Mrs. Boykin was dedicated to healthy stress-free living. Lillie Dillie didn't like stress, either. Lillie Dillie had had her share of stress in her personal life. Stress came often whenever she walked to the market. Lillie Dillie felt a lot of stress and dreaded passing by Mr. Rockwaller's pit bull dogs. Three fenced-in pit bull dogs jumped against the silver fence, barking fiercely at Lillie Dillie. Lillie Dillie stared straight and walked as far away from the dogs as she could. Butterflies fluttered in her stomach and she was scared. She would say over and over, "I don't fear anything. The dogs can't hurt me. I can do this! What dogs can stop a fearless Lillie Dillie?"

Intra-Comprehension Questions (ICQ) Why must we face our fears? What actions are you taking to walk through your fears? Will you stay stuck in a rut?

When Lillie Dillie arrived at the market, she asked Mrs. Peppersnicker for a cool chocolate covered strawberry to calm her fears. Then Lillie Dillie used one of Mrs. Peppersnicker's baskets to fill it with fruits, juices, and fresh cinnamon. She paid Mrs. Peppersnicker and headed back to Mrs. Boykin. Lillie Dillie carefully packed away Mrs. Boykin's change which was a nickel.

Again, Lillie Dillie dreaded passing by the pit bulls as she returned to Mrs. Boykin's big white house. Again, all three dogs were jumping against the silver fence and barking like mad dogs. Again, Lillie Dillie was saying positive things to help her walk through the emotions of fear. "I will not fear dogs that are fenced in. I'm never scared. I walk by these dogs twice a week. They can't touch me. I'm moving forward anyway." When Lillie Dillie arrived and set the bag of vegetables and cinnamon on the kitchen table, Mrs. Boykin told Lillie Dillie "calm down and rest and I'll make us fruity smoothies." Lillie Dillie placed the nickel on the table by the goods. Lillie Dillie relaxed and gazed at the golden brown tea cakes that were on the table. Tea cakes are not sugary. In fact, tea cakes taste like biscuits with sugar and spices in them. Tea cakes are great with smoothies or tea. At last, Lillie Dillie enjoyed a fruity smoothie and a tea cake. She carried one of her tea cakes to her friend named Pudgy.

Intra-Comprehension Questions (ICQ) What is your image of Pudgy? Is obesity a common problem of kids today? How can it be conquered?

Pudgy was round and thick-boned. Pudgy was obese and ate more than he should for a kid his age. Pudgy was allowed to eat three pork chops with every refill of his plate until Mr. Buckeye said enough is enough. He asked Pudgy "what can you do to stop your habit of overeating? What decision can you make to stop students from teasing you about your weight?" Pudgy thought about these questions. Then Pudgy said:

1) I can consult the school nurse about fats in the foods that I eat.
2) I can write what I am eating and how often I am eating.
3) I can change the types of food, my portions of food, and the time that I eat.
4) I can use my words to say, "I feel sad when you tease me about my weight. Would you please stop making fun of my size and my name? Please call me Pudgy with all jokes aside?"

Pudgy told his father that he was working on a plan to get his weight under control. Pudgy was so proud to have a father to give him challenges to help him. Pudgy was also happy to have a father present and engaged in the spiritual and financial prosperity of the Buckeye family. Pudgy was more proud of his father than anyone in the school. Mr. Buckeye wore the pants in his home. He was honored in his family. Mr. Buckeye was proud of Pudgy, too. Mr. Buckeye laid his hands on his son's shoulders and said, "Son, I accept you as you are. I love you and I expect you to do greater things than I did. And I pray that you accept the love from the Greater One."

Intra-Comprehension Questions (ICQ) What does "honor" mean? How do you honor your father? How do you honor whoever is the head of the home you live in?

When Mr. Buckeye told Pudgy to do chores before homework, Pudgy answered, "Yes, Sir." Pudgy never talked back to his father or his mother. Respect and honesty were highly valued by the Buckeyes. Honesty was the only policy in this family, too.

Mr. Buckeye placed ten nickels which were Pudgy's allowance on the wooden kitchen table and told Pudgy to count the money out aloud. Mr. Buckeye taught Pudgy to pay his tithes or one nickel out of his fifty cents to support the work that the church does in the community. Mr. Buckeye also taught Pudgy to save at least a nickel out of every fifty cents that he earned. He would say, "Son, don't let money burn a whole in your pocket. Save some money so you will have a sunny day when everyone else is having a rainy day."

Mr. Buckeye taught Pudgy how to set up a simple budget. An example is as follows:

Income

Allowance of	50 cents

Expenses

STWCI Church	5 cents
Save	5 cents
Lunch Box Snacks	30 cents
Hold for A Need	<u>10 cents</u>
Total	50 cents

You can see that Pudgy learned how to pay tithes and save money at an early age. This is a good habit for you to start. Put a book mark on this page. Get a piece of paper and take time to set up a budget that fits your allowance or salary. Share more money and save more money, if you are able to. If you are feeling like you are not earning enough money to budget, model after this fifty cents budget. Learn the principle of saving money early in life. Once you have formed the habit of saving a little money, save greater amounts of money when you begin to increase your income.

Intra-Comprehension Questions (ICQ) Is Pudgy spending more than his allowance amount? Does this mean that he is living within his means or spending under the amount of his allowance? Explain how you will live within your means.

Prosperity feels better than poverty any day. Some people say that they have been poor. Some people say that they have been rich. Most people say that rich feels better. Being rich allows you to have enough money to help someone else have a better life. The money will take on the character of the owner. Remember that.

Remember Lillie Dillie did not have a father helping her develop early budgeting skills. However, she listened to Pudgy and Pudgy showed her his budget. She copied his model of a budget. She earned money running errands and began to budget that money. When Mr. Buckeye would volunteer in schools and share stories about how the Buckeyes don't waste money; and the Buckeyes don't buy things that go to waste. We only buy things of no good taste, he would say.

Lillie Dillie would sit, and stare with glazing eyes as she focused on every word that Mr. Buckeye spoke.

Even though Lillie Dillie admired all of the concepts that Mr. Buckeye taught, she would sometimes still spend money that she got from her mother, Ms. Helen. She would buy a pork chop plate. Essie Mae's was a café that Lillie Dillie looked forward to going to on the first of the month when her mother received her social security check. This treat was important to Lillie Dillie because there were times when her family did not have food to eat. There were times when the electricity was cut off. Ms. Helen would burn kerosene lamps and get small food items on credit at Robinson's Grocery Store. Ms. Helen would pay her grocery bill as soon as her social security check came in. She knew how to build a fire, place cooking oil in a black, cast iron skillet, and fry chicken outside. Ms. Helen would build a fire and prop an iron rack over the fire each time that the electricity was cut off. Picture an iron rack stacked on bricks and the rack placed over the fire. Keep visualizing oil heating in the skillet. Ms. Helen placed flour in a bag and threw the chicken in the bag to coat it. She gripped the bag and shook it. Then she carefully placed the chicken wings and drumsticks in the skillet. Things are so modern now. That was so much fun and the chicken was delicious. Lillie Dillie was full of joy as long as she had her family. As the food was cooking, Lillie Dillie would keep herself entertained. She would plunder through the yard collecting lady bugs. They were her special friends. She also made mud cakes by taking dirt out of the field and mixing the dirt with water. She cooked greens which were really wild plants that grew in a field. These were pretend side dishes for the family to eat with the chicken. Lillie Dillie did not realize that her family was considered poor. She was happy, full of joy and that was all that mattered to her.

There were special times when Lillie Dillie had a special Sunday meal cooked by Ms. Helen. She fried chicken, boiled pinto beans, made red drink and baked home-made banana pudding. Those were the days. Lillie Dillie was the baby of the family and was treated special even though the family did not have a lot of money. Mrs. Boykin used to buy Lillie Dillie dresses and press Lillie Dillie's hair. Lillie Dillie cherished a special picture that showed one of her favorite dresses that Mrs. Boykin had bought. Mrs. Boykin made Lillie Dillie's hair shine for the picture, too. Lillie Dillie's mother, brothers, older friends, aunts, and other relatives did special things for Lillie Dillie. They all were available to talk to her about anything and any problems. Ask her and she could tell you many stories if you asked her. Her brothers still tell her that she is "special." Lillie Dillie was appreciated because she loved to help people. She comforted friends who were feeling down. She welcomed new kids to their neighborhood and school. She did not let kids who teased her get in the way of being who she really is. Her values were deeply rooted in the Higher One. Therefore, she did not have to please everybody.

Intra-Comprehension Questions (ICQ) How are you defining your "beauty"? Are you beautiful on the inside and inside? What can you improve?

Let the beauty within you be seen on the outside of you. People should be pleased to be with you. If that is not your story, fix it. People feel happier when you are a positive person. It is unfortunate that there seems to be more negative people in the world than positive people. Lillie Dillie made it a habit to be resilient. She refused to stay in a low emotional state of mind. She might cry one night. Oh, but the next morning, she was working on praying, talking to the Most High, writing about her feelings, writing positive sayings, and she topped off controlling her emotions with singing uplifting songs. She will share with you how silly she can get, too. If there is a part of you that you want to change, change it. You have the power to become whoever you want to become. Helping other people is a good way to feel good about whom you are becoming. If you are bitter, let the bitterness go. Lillie Dillie made a vow not to lash out at people who hurt her. One part of her so badly wanted to be mean. Then the better side of her would say, "I don't want to hurt anyone. If I hurt them then I have to apologize." She would angrily dig her dirt for her mud cakes. She would smash her mud cakes and twist them in her hands. She had a habit of saying, "I love Pudgy with his round self," if Pudgy were the person she was angry with. She would repeat over and over, "I love Pudgy. I love Pudgy." Then when she saw Pudgy, it was easier to talk to him. Here is what Lillie Dillie did that was so silly. She would blast her music. She would put on five dresses and dance really big to "The Multiplication Shake" CD. She would be shaking up and down and turning all around making silly faces. She would throw her over-dressed body on the couch, start laughing hilariously, and roll on to the floor. Wasn't that silly? She forgot that she was ever angry or bitter. Wouldn't you say Lillie Dillie could get quite silly? She would win the battle again, forgive, and refuse to stay angry. She refused to lash out and seek revenge. This character made her such a special little girl, too. This special girl had people she trusted and she talked to them. She asked for ways to approach people and ways to mediate peacefully. She faced her problems without hurting the other person. She valued being able to communicate after the conflict was resolved.

Intra-Comprehension Questions (ICQ) What do you do to release your anger or bitterness? Do you think about how you will feel after you hurt someone? Do you think about how the other person will feel after you hurt their feelings?

Lillie Dillie's Adolescent Years

Lillie Dillie spent her childhood going to the store for old people and was rewarded a silver quarter, a fruity smoothie, and golden tea cakes. Lillie Dillie spent some of her money and she budgeted a few times, but this inconsistency causes greater problems and will cause problems for Lillie Dillie for many years. Her inconsistency in handling money causes her to still need Mr. Buckeye's money management advice. Later in the chapter, she will wish that she had listened at an early age. Another issue in the adolescent years of Lillie Dillie, is her wrong choice of friends. She steered away from some of her values.

Lillie Dillie attended Linear Jr. High School. She tried out for the cheerleader squad twice. Each time she couldn't get her coordination together. Chanting a cheer and moving her arms and legs simultaneously just couldn't vive. Lillie Dillie's intellect was more intact than her physical coordination. Lillie Dillie was voted smartest girl in her class. This accomplishment didn't satisfy Lillie Dillie. She wanted to be known as the most chic and fashionable girl. She started seeking friends who were from rich families and had the best of clothes. She wanted to dress like the girls who had chic jeans and stilettos from Italy. Lillie Dillie's mom had struggles paying her electric bill. How in the world did she think that she was going to buy some chic jeans and stilettos?

 Some foolish company mailed Lillie Dillie a credit card with a $2,000 limit on it with a 19% interest rate. It was foolish to give a student who had no job a credit card. Lillie Dillie bought over $500 worth of clothes and over $200 worth of accessories and could not pay for all of that debt. Lillie Dillie was trying to be in the "in crowd" with the rich girls. They did not care about her. They knew that she could not afford those clothes that she had charged. Whatever the rich girls planned, Lillie Dillie said, "Count me in." She had to charge her tickets to go to the dinner theaters, the movie theatres, the orchestra performances, etc. Imagine paying 19% interest on entertainment. That was outright dumb. That credit card company had another thing coming if they thought that Ms. Helen was going to pay Lillie Dillie's debt off for her. Ms. Helen firmly told Lillie Dillie, "I didn't make the debt and I'm not paying the debt."

Lillie Dillie felt a noose around her neck during junior high and high school years. She felt a big knot in her throat and her stomach got butterflies in it. The anguish of overwhelming debt felt terrible. Lillie Dillie lost her interest in her stiletto shoes when she got her first monthly statement from the credit card company. She didn't know how she was going to pay the creditor and that 19% interest rate didn't make things any easier. Stress made her back and neck sting. Lillie Dillie was engulfed with stress and pain.

Intra-Comprehension Questions (ICQ) What should the one (1) credit card that you own be used for? What interest rates are next best to 0% interest? What is the problem with 19%? Are the clothes and accessories assets or liabilities? Explain.

Mr. Turner, Lillie Dillie's teacher, noticed that Lillie Dillie had begun to stare into space a lot and day dream in class. Or in agony, Lillie Dillie cried "Oh, oh, how in the world am I going to get out of this mess? If only I could start over. I would be satisfied with the good grades. I would have stayed buddies with Pudgy who could care less about show off clothes." Mr. Turner had to snap his fingers in Lillie Dillie's face as he stood directly in front of her. He said, "Snap back into reality, Lillie Dillie. Your grades are dropping since you have started to space out in class. Come talk to me after class." Things began to go downhill for Lillie Dillie. She was sick from the stress of high debt and no income. Mr. Buckeye had told her about high debt to low income. He told her that having more debt than income will keep one from getting a loan for a first-time home. She had to do worse than that and attain all of that debt and no income.

Lillie Dillie's addiction to impressing everyone got her in a world of trouble this time. The truth was, Lillie Dillie was so insecure about her appearance that she hid it by dressing so flashy. She would have come out better getting free counseling from our guidance counselor. She needed to build her self-esteem by talking about how to love herself better. She could have learned to make positive confessions about herself. She could have helped someone else have a better life and that would have helped her, too. She would have been nourishing her own soul by helping someone else. Oh yes, there were simpler things to do to build her self-confidence than get in bad debt. Now, Lillie Dillie has wars in her mind because of her choice to be an exuberant shopper. To add to the financial crash, she was forced to think back to the day that she bought a friend a pair of jeans on her credit card while she was still unemployed. Her friend said, "I sure would be happy if you could get those jeans with my initials on them just this one time for me." Lillie Dillie volunteered her credit card and said, "Sure, why not?" Lillie Dillie has not heard from that friend since they went shopping. Some friend, huh?

Intra-Comprehension Questions (ICQ) How could Lillie Dillie have said, "NO" to her friend? Should you have to buy friendship? Create and role-play this shopping day scene.

Things got worse for Lillie Dillie because some new neighbors moved beside Lillie Dillie at the end of her senior year. The teens wore name brand clothes and shoes. Well, Lillie Dillie went into high gear trying to look like she was all that, again. She kept charging and faking it until she had to go to work every evening after high school classes. The credit card company started to call her early in the morning asking for payments. Lillie Dillie would bury her head under her pillow every time that phone would ring early in the morning. She told Ms. Helen to tell them, "I'm not here." Ms. Helen just gave her the dark eye and said, "Talk to these people. You made your bed hard. Now, lay in it. You are going to learn the hard way."

After school that day, Lillie Dillie had to go to the Lee and Grocery for a job. This was the store that she used to run errands to for the elderly when she was a little girl. Mr. Terry made Lillie Dillie talk about the choices that she had made. He gave her a look of disbelief. He told Lillie Dillie that his mother told him "don't buy what you can't pay for." This meant do not charge anything. Do without stuff. Stuff won't last. Mr. Terry explained her job description. He allowed Lillie Dillie to work and scolded her for not listening to Mr. Buckeye. All through the school year, the summer, Lillie Dillie's senior year, and her first year in college, Lillie Dillie had to work to pay off her bad credit card debt. Debt is easy to get into and hard to get out of. Overwhelming debt follows some people for 20 to 30 years. Mr. Buckeye had told her a true story about a man who hoarded all kinds of gold chains. He had about 10 credit cards and traveled around the world collecting gold chains. The man didn't make enough money to pay all of those credit cards. He had to get debt counseling and messed up his credit reputation. When he needed a loan for a home, he couldn't get it. He thought back to his wants or lust for gold chains. He had to face the fact that his wants outweighed his needs. You see, you become a servant to your bad habits. That applies to any bad habits. The man had to rent an apartment and was not able to partake in home ownership.

Mr. Buckeye stopped by Lee and Terry Grocery and asked Lillie Dillie to come by his office later to set up a budget and a plan to project the credit card pay off. Of course, Lillie Dillie accepted. She was ready to listen now. Imagine all of the years that passed by. Lillie Dillie was broke and broken. She had learned lessons that would affect the rest of her life. As long as she had nothing other than the Lee and Terry Grocery salary, she couldn't spend what she didn't have. She struggled at work and struggled to graduate from high school. She had to wear what she had. She had to wear the stilettos to sweep the floor. Those heels have no place on a job in the grocery store. The rich girls came in the store on purpose. They snickered behind Lillie Dillie's back. One said, "I told you she couldn't afford those clothes and accessories she was charging. Now, look at her."

Lillie Dillie's College Years

Lillie Dillie survived the ridicule. She prepared for her first year in college. She was still conscious of her image. She wanted to impress the guys in college now. She had gone shopping for some new clothes. She wanted to still charge on her 19% credit card. Several young men admired Lillie Dillie. She was looking for the rich guy who had some money and a promising future. She felt that he could help her pay her bad debt balances off and she could start using his credit cards. Lillie Dillie did not get these principles from Ms. Helen. Lillie Dillie manipulated her way to be seen by the guys who were from a wealthy background. She played pool in the recreation room, if the rich guys were in the recreation room. She was strategically placing herself so that Mr. Right could see her. She had her eyes on a guy and did not know his name. She asked guys in the cafeteria who is that muscular guy with that round hair cut? Where did he come from?

"The Bam" was who she was seeking out. He thought that Lillie Dillie was the cutest girl on the campus. He didn't quite know every detail about her. He knew that he had to take time to get to know her. His mother had told him to get a good education and do not bring any babies back home. Even though he knew about her past of impressing others and impulsive spending habits, he would spend the money that his mother had mailed him on chicken and pop for Lillie Dillie. They used go to Spivey's Chicken and buy some spicy chicken and then they would playfully roll down the grassy hills of Grambling State University. They did anything to be close to each other. The Bam loved Lillie Dillie at first sight. However, he couldn't marry Lillie Dillie until she straightened out her bad motives, her bad spending habits, and her bad credit history. The Bam knew that his family would not be happy about him inheriting Lillie Dillie's debt. And they would not live happily ever after until Lillie Dillie made some changes in her life style choices.

The Bam proposed to Lillie Dillie with the stipulation that "you must pay off the credit card debt, late fees, and NSF or non-sufficient funds charges that are attached to your checking account before we can set a wedding date." Lillie Dillie had a payday loan with a high interest rate to pay, too. Lillie Dillie could not get excited about her wedding gown and her wedding ceremony because her bad debt had turned into an American nightmare. She had created a debt monster that was a hindrance to her marriage. She began projecting pay offs of each debt. She was amazed when she saw that with consistency and hard work, she really could pay off her bad debts. Mr. Buckeye's teachings were super valuable now.

Intra-Comprehension Questions (ICQ) Will you learn from Lillie Dillie's dilemma or mistakes to avoid bad debt in your youthful years? Will you be a valuable asset to your future spouse? Explain your plan.

Lillie Dillie wouldn't file bankruptcy even though she wanted to pay the bad debt off quickly. She knew that filing bankruptcy was not going to work with a nice guy like The Bam. It wouldn't work for several reasons. The Bam and his family would not accept her being irresponsible and unaccountable for the choices she had made. She felt so regretful about the financial mess that she had made. Her new in-laws wouldn't accept that she lied to the creditors about being able to pay them back their money. Lillie Dillie knew that the legal fees for filing bankruptcy had increased and there were a lot of financial counseling classes that she would have to take. Therefore, she worked in the evenings and on Saturdays in order to pay off all of her debts. Lillie Dillie was feeling like "it was so easy to get in debt and now I feel like a slave struggling to pay for my outlandish spending habits." On top of that, she can't get married until the debt is gone. Lillie Dillie was warring in her mind again. In her mind she wishing it was all over. She had to face feeling obligated to years of paying out the debt for clothes that she did not own anymore. She was thinking, "I can't tithe or give to any one for any cause. When I get another chance, I won't blow it." She was angry and thinking I don't even want another credit card. She vowed, "I won't waste my money once I get out of this mess." Lillie Dillie was tired of her twisted thinking. She thought that because she was young, she had time to mess up. She had no idea that her looks alone would not get her a husband. She had no idea that a man would not marry her until she paid off her debt.

Lillie Dillie did something about her situation. She labored hard to get her man. She started tracking her payments in her checkbook register. She started tracking her payments and balances on another tracking form. Several years passed. Lillie Dillie and The Bam kept dating through this process. He was a strong young man and did not go back on his decision. As Lillie Dillie began to pay her debts before the due date, her FICO or credit score began to get higher. Mr. Buckeye had told Lillie Dillie and a class of seniors back in high school to set goals about not wasting money and paying bills ahead of time so that their credit score would be over 700. It was a good thing that Mr. Buckeye had taken time to give educational seminars. His teachings were making more sense to Lillie Dillie. The Bam's father had taught him not to waste money and to pay his bills ahead of time. Lillie Dillie was playing catch up. She didn't have a father figure in her home.

Mr. Buckeye had told Lillie Dillie to track each ACH or Automatic Clearing House payment that was deducted out of her checking account. He emphasized that she should be sure to deduct that payment from her current checkbook balance. There was also great emphasis in keeping money in her checking account for the outstanding checks and financial transactions that had not yet been paid. As the years of tracking paid off, Lillie Dillie was excited about the day that she paid her last credit card payment. She started singing and dancing and rolling on the floor. She mailed the payment and attached a letter requesting that the company send her a written letter of confirmation that she indeed had paid them off. She also asked them to close out the account as of the beginning of the pay off date.

Lillie Dillie wanted the letter for her records and for The Bam. She set up a file so that she could find her proof that she had paid the bill. She did not want to get in future arguments with that company if they tried to continue to collect payments from her. She visited her credit union for a debit card application. She had to get her first ever debit card number also so that she could begin a new habit of paying for her needs. She did not want to be a slave to wants ever again.

Lillie Dillie's mistakes in life influences smart readers to live a life of right motives, right dealings, and rightfully helping other people. These choices were much easier to live through than all the drama that Lillie Dillie survived.

Lillie Dillie submitted an email to the payday loan company notifying them that she was paying them off and closing out the account. Lillie Dillie paid with an electronic payment. Lillie Dillie asked the loan company to send her a letter of confirmation saying that they had received the electronic payment and the account was closed as of a specific date. Lillie Dillie was advised by Mr. Buckeye to print a hard copy of the receipt and file the copy for her records. They also made an electronic folder and saved the electronic receipt in the electronic folder. Mr. Buckeye told her to write down the email, username, and password for future reference. He knew of times he had forgotten which email he had sent business emails through. He knew that computer systems crash and lose records, too. Lillie Dillie listened to Mr. Buckeye and filed hard copies of notification letters, confirmation letters, and receipts.

Mr. Buckeye made Lillie Dillie aware that employers sometimes look at your credit history and your credit or FICO score in order to decide if your character will fit their company. Imagine facing a desired employer after they have seen your poor credit scores. He reminded her that credit scores may also determine what mortgage or car loans one can or cannot be granted and will determine how high interest rates will be on a loan. He told Lillie Dillie to be aware of the status of her credit score with:

- over 760 or above being an 'A'

- above 700 , a 'B'

- between 600 and 700, a 'C'

- below 600 is a 'D' or even an 'F'

Be assured that the low scores will cause higher interest rates. Mr. Buckeye strongly encouraged Lillie Dillie to identify the three companies that keep records or keep track of people's monthly payments to their creditors. The three reporting agencies or companies are Equifax, Experian, and Trans Union, and will send you your credit score as often as you request it. He told her that debt that is much higher than her income will also stop her from getting a mortgage or car loan. Loan companies refer to it as "debt to income ratios."

Intra-Comprehension Questions (ICQ) What score do you want your potential employer to find in your report? What is the contact information for each of the reporting agencies? Use www.google.com to research for more information by typing the names of the agencies in the search box.

Image problems decreased. After Lillie Dillie had cleaned up her bad credit history, she was not so into image as she once was. The Bam and Lillie Dillie sat down and set their date and discussed their family plans. Then they had a simple wedding and became pregnant immediately. She kept going to college. Lillie Dillie didn't value name brand baby clothes anymore. She would not argue about what their first baby would wear. Lillie Dillie was reminded of her college loans and the need to refinance for a lower interest rate. When The Bam and Lillie Dillie applied for an apartment, Lillie Dillie's education loan payment affected where they could live. They didn't have jobs that paid enough for them to pay upfront three months of rent for a really classy apartment. The apartment manager told them that their monthly earnings together had to equal three months of rent. They said, "Yeah, right." They moved on to a more reasonable apartment manager. Real life was hitting both of them really hard. They had to live in some apartments that were somewhat run down. It was good that Lillie Dillie didn't need to show off. At one time, Lillie Dillie would not have thought about living in a shack. She had really been broken and humbled.

Lillie Dillie had to take a reality check. When the baby needed some diapers, Lillie Dillie had to put herself second. When the baby needed some food and medicine, Lillie Dillie had to put herself second again. If The Bam was ever going to buy their first starter home, high debt to low or no income could never be their reality as a married couple. Lillie Dillie had begun to see that it was mandatory for unnecessary shopping to stop on their joint credit card in order to be approved for a home loan. Grambling, Louisiana was small. Therefore, they could get around the town without a car easily at least for a while.

Mr. Buckeye met with the newlyweds. Before they got into a deep discussion, Mr. Buckeye prayed that their eyes would be opened and their understanding enlightened. He educated the couple about the laws related to credit cards and bankruptcy and other strict regulations. One law required that minimum payments be doubled, and one law approved of universal default which made you pay interest rates like 29% on all of your cards, if you were late paying one payment on only one card. Filing bankruptcy was more difficult and required a high number of credit counseling classes to take and fees to file bankruptcy were higher.

Mr. Buckeye informed the young couple not to pay a variable interest rate, nor to make interest-only or minimum payments when they finally decided to buy a starter home. He warned them that some years down the road, that the loan company would "recast" if they took the easy route and paid the minimum payment on a mortgage loan. Recast means that the loan company would require or mandate a large monthly payment and would not allow the interest only or minimum payments any more. He told them that they would both be struggling trying to meet that home note, utility bills, and high gasoline prices. Mr. Buckeye had several budget concepts to share with the couple. He had some numbers and pictures of positive abundance, positive scarcity, and negative scarcity to show the young couple. Positive abundance was a life style of tithing, saving, cash investing, real estate ownership, and being able to pay good debts off monthly or pay cash for cars easily. It also included a vacation that was paid for in cash. Positive scarcity was a life style of tithing, limited saving, and the bills were paid with a very little extra money left over. Lastly, negative scarcity was a life style that made people stop paying tithes because they had too much debt for the low income they earned. This was the life style where people didn't have food some days and they used toilet paper as their kitchen paper towels, too. Electricity and water were sometimes cut off. This life style horrified The Bam and Lillie Dillie.

Mr. Buckeye shared ways that the newlyweds could build wealth and allowed them to choose the one that best fit them. First, Mr. Buckeye stressed the need for spiritual development and discipline before they could attain wealth. Mr. Buckeye told Lillie Dillie that the Most High could help her change her mentality about spending money wastefully and impressing people. He said that the Most High could also give her strength to discipline herself to save more money. Mr. Buckeye advised the couple to call and ask their local credit union or bank about a free financial advisor. And then go in and ask for expert's advice about various cash investments. Mr. Buckeye knew that if the newlyweds saved thousands of dollars by not over paying interest on their mortgage loan, they could take those savings and build wealth. This means that when someone buys a home and pays interest rather than principal, they lose money. He knew that if the newlyweds were aware of and used a system to accelerate the building of equity, cancelling interest, and paying back less interest to the mortgage lender, they could invest in more real estate property and build wealth. Mr. Buckeye knew that Lillie Dillie and The Bam had the potential to be entrepreneurs. He shared with Lillie Dillie how she could take her life story and put it in motivational speeches and books and sell a very inspirational product. The Bam on the other hand had great mathematical skills that could help someone manage money better. He could advise guys and girls not to marry someone who possessed a lot of debt. A lot of bad debt shows that a person has some inner issues and is not ever satisfied. Lillie Dillie liked hearing about how to build wealth with her life story. She was not excited about having to admit that she had to get rid of her debt and her bad motives. That was not anything to be proud of. She knew that if anyone really understood the budget concept of negative scarcity, they would stop bad habits immediately. Anyway, she could not accept negative scarcity in her life.

Lillie Dillie refused negative scarcity. Lillie Dillie bucked her eyes and said, "I have lived a hard childhood life and it wasn't all by my choice. I admit I have also made my own bad choices just a few years ago. I will not choose negative scarcity for my child". Lillie Dillie asked Mr. Buckeye to show them a budget that could work for them and they wanted to pass early money management skills throughout the generations to follow them. The budget excluded bad credit card debt, late charges, non-sufficient funds charges, and pay day loans. Because Mr. Buckeye was able to show the couple how to budget wisely, they escaped living a life of negative scarcity. Seeing the bigger picture of a better life helped Lillie Dillie and The Bam strive for a better life. Lillie Dillie took a deep breath. The Bam just looked at her. He knew that he could make the change that he needed to for the family. Lillie Dillie had to scratch her head and decide to change her mind set about her impulsive spending habits. She had to ignore great sales days. She could not afford to "think" and say "I'm going to catch my last sale and then I'm going to save some money for real." A lot of people say what they will do and don't do as they say but will do as they "think". They do what they think about consistently. As a man thinks so is he. Lillie Dillie did not want The Bam to divorce her because she had fallen back into her old habits. He didn't marry her when she had the bad habits.

Lillie Dillie hung up pictures of a family that lived in "negative scarcity" and that helped her to live life by design and not from crisis to crisis. Lillie Dillie was willing to start with positive scarcity and advance to positive abundance. The Bam and Lillie Dillie knew that they were going to have to pray and do some things they had never done to get some things that they had never had. Financial freedom and time freedom seemed to be common goals of each. Materialism had already gotten Lillie Dillie in trouble. Both of them were ready for a spiritual make over.

Mr. Buckeye invited The Bam and Lillie Dillie to church. They accepted the invitation to church and began to listen intensively for new directions for their lives. Mr. Buckeye told them that it was going to take will power. And it was something that they could do. He counseled them and helped them set up new goals and action steps to change their income status. Mr. Buckeye guaranteed the couple that working spiritual principles in their lives would help them to become financially free. Mr. Buckeye told them value right living and of course, discipline, work, budgeting, and saving were spiritual principles that the young couple had to master. The couple learned how to schedule time to make their daily confessions. Mr. Buckeye typed up these confessions and gave them to the couple. They were as follows:

1) We will do what is right even when we don't want to.
2) We will be thankful for what we have.
3) We will walk through fearful things.
4) We will be happy with what we have.
5) We will be disciplined even when we are tempted to shop.
6) We will be wise and save for the future.
7) We will have great wealth and be happy with it.

Their strategic action plan began with attainable goals and with positive affirmations that they believed they could achieve. The Bam and Lillie Dillie loved the positive affirmation that said, "We shall have great wealth and be happy with it." Both of them worked smart and hard. Lillie Dillie finished college, worked her passion in a business, and knocked herself out helping people reach their life goals. She established a home-based business and showed people how to make a living doing what they loved to do. Lillie Dillie wrote a book and drew from her life experiences. Daily, she was invited to speak from the book that she had authored. Lillie Dillie had become an entrepreneur, a professional, certified presenter of her own book. She could not speak at all of those engagements. Lillie Dillie began to make an abundance of money, live the real positive abundant life, and no longer had to fake having the best in life. The Bam finished college and refinanced his education loan and paid the debt in a timely manner. He tracked the payments of his loans so that he would not be charged twice. He heard that some companies collect repetitive payments if you do not keep track of each payment and project pay off dates. The Bam worked in his passion as a financial analyst seven hours a day. He too, loved helping people make wise money decisions. He donated one Saturday each month to offer free financial counseling to poor people. He worked one hour each evening trading stocks. He had money available to buy the right tools to help him invest wisely in stocks. He mentored a few self-motivated self-starters in how to trade stocks. They even drove to Texas to attend professional seminars. He did not over book himself.

The Bam was a good father. He spent a lot of time with their first born, Braidee. He was present and available to help raise his child. He treated Lillie Dillie like the queen that she had become. He actually enjoyed leading his family in spiritual devotions. He made sure that Lillie Dillie placed tithes and offerings at the top of their budget. He took time to make sure that his family was protected. He

bought protection for his family. He had money deducted from his pay check
for life insurance, medical and dental insurance. The Bam's father had taught
him the importance of buying life insurance to make sure that his family was
taken care of after death. He bought medical insurance to make
sure that medical catastrophes did not burden the family while he was alive. He
had heard horror stories about how medical debts caused family years of
struggle. Even though The Bam knew about stocks, he was open to keeping
abreast of stock updates. He believed in going through the process of
averaging higher than 12% with his stocks if he invested over a span of years.
Because The Bam and Lillie Dillie were earning more money, they both were
interested in hearing about several options. They sought information about how
to buy undeveloped land, gold, commodities, malls, and banks in the future.
Their goal was to make money work for them. Then The Bam and Lillie Dillie
discussed what companies they wanted to invest in. The Bam and Lillie Dillie
were prepared to move out of their rundown apartment into a 300-unit
apartment complex that they joined income together and purchased. The
planned was to occupy one of the units. They hired a property management
company to take care of the property. They were happy that their credit scores
were high and they could reap the benefits of being in ownership. They
charged their tenants fairly and used the collections to pay the mortgage for
the 300-unit purchase. Lending institutions were willing to take a risk with this
couple that had become such high income earners and were now a great risk
for lenders.

This couple was a prime example of what can happen when you truly learn
from your mistakes. They were an example of how changing your mind set
changes your life. Lillie Dillie had poor concepts about how to use money. She
chose to accept Mr. Buckeye's mentorship to help her change her belief about
how to use money. We can believe that The Bam's refusal to marry her under
the wrong circumstances also influenced Lillie Dillie to change her motives and
poor money management habits. This couple worked wealth principles for
years. Mr. Buckeye was in their lives to stay. They were also confident that their
services, products, and experiences could benefit the people in the world. They
set up their legal business structures with top notch business plans, marketed and
sold their services and products. They kept their wealth moving and growing.
They had the support of a team because they know that no man is an island.
And best of all they gave back to the community time, money, and information
to help people change their spiritual and financial directions of their lives. They

had a "gift fund" to help victims of unexpected catastrophes. This is a couple that stayed the course and currently lives a very prosperous life. They are excited about helping the next generation build generational wealth. They are changing the way people think about wasting money. People value money and making it work for them.

Intra-Comprehension Questions (ICQ) Have you written your life's goals and plans so that you have clear directions for your life? Are you willing invest in what you believe in? Do you have the right people in your life to help you get where you are going?

Extra Credit: Fill in the blank.

Money is _____.

I can use more money to _____.

Positive beliefs will help you move forward in reaching your financial goals. Negative beliefs will stagnate you. Find a mentor and save yourself from the school of financial hard knocks. Mentors may be books, DVDs, videos, movies, or accessible people, etc. Establish the work of your hands by doing what you do excellently. You must work in order to fulfill your destiny. Work is not a choice. You must work. Combining your work and passion is the smartest move you can make. Entrepreneurship is ideal for courageous people who refuse to work for employers. For people who feel that they don't want to be the boss, go to work daily and on time. Put in quality time and handle conflicts professionally. Never get mad at the boss and quit the job. Stay the course and grow. If you don't work, don't expect to have food handed to you.

The Bam and Lillie Dillie were great examples of taking your best person to the work. They were passionate about providing services to people. Be reminded that Lillie Dillie was afraid to get caught in a negative scarcity life style. Intentionally, put action to your passion and progress towards positive abundance. Remember to help someone else and you will have accomplished a lot. Remember to look at pictures of negative scarcity if you are tempted to be wasteful and impulsive. Lillie Dillie said if she could have seen the end at the beginning, she would have better financial choices.

Visualize pictures of negative scarcity which include:

1) your dollars going down the drain
2) fighting with your spouse because there is not enough money for bills
3) your checkbook registry is in the red and you have no money for bills
4) you're seated in the doctor's office stressed out to the max with your hands on your forehead worried to death about lack of money for bills
5) near having a heart attack
6) no brand foods in your kitchen or no food in your kitchen
7) no clean clothes to wear to a job interview
8) spot clean clothes daily because you can't afford dry cleaning bills
9) using toilet tissue to drain oil off your fried chicken instead of paper towels
10) catching a ride with your boss because you have no money for gas for your car
11) sleeping on a roll away bed
12) eating mayonnaise sandwiches with no meat
13) using a box and ice for your refrigerator
14) never having anything to share with others

Intra-Comprehension Questions (ICQ) Did the visualization influence you not to waste money? Did the visualizations influence you not to be lazy and not to refuse work?

Change what you can. Make your money work for you. Do not choose negative scarcity as your end.

Lillie Dillie Reigns in Parenthood

Lillie Dillie becomes a wow mother! Lillie Dillie's life experiences, mistakes, mother, and aunt helped her to become the best mother ever. After you read all of the areas that Lillie Dillie covered to help their baby girl live a life of *"skipping poverty and starting wealthy"*, you will say, "wow!" The Bam and Lillie Dillie had a daughter named Braidee who was raised with a lot of love and discipline. Lillie Dillie set up a schedule that included family devotions, chores, and family fun activities. The family devotion was led by The Bam three times during the week. On the day of midweek church service and Sundays, The Bam did not lead the family in family devotion because he drove the family to church. When there were family devotions, they began with a prayer. Each family member took a turn to pray or simply give thanks to God. Two to three favorite songs were sung. And then the family read a chapter from the bible which was usually Proverbs. The chapter matched the date of the month. If it were the 3rd day of the month, the family read chapter three of Proverbs. Lillie Dillie really believed that instilling a love for God and building a strong relationship with God in the home were keys to life's successes. Lillie Dillie would always tell Braidee that having good character would help her to do the right thing even when she didn't want to. Lillie Dillie used to tell stories to Braidee about times when Godly character helped her to do right on her job. Once Lillie Dillie did not like a secretary on her job. She didn't tell the secretary that she didn't like her. However, she knew in her heart that she didn't like the secretary. When Secretary's Day came, Lillie Dillie bought the secretary an extremely nice gift. The secretary was so appreciative and Lillie Dillie gained a new friend. Afterwards, Lillie Dillie was so glad that she had gained a new friend by just buying a gift that she dreaded buying for a secretary she once despised. The power to give and make someone else happy was so fulfilling for Lillie Dillie. The secretary and Lillie Dillie developed a genuine, life-long relationship.

Lillie Dillie remembered that obesity was a problem of her childhood friend, Pudgy. Therefore, she made sure that Braidee did not overeat. Lillie Dillie fed her family balanced meals and age-appropriate portions. Braidee enjoyed eating brain snacks such as muffins and grain bars. Often, Lillie Dillie baked meats, vegetable casseroles, and served wheat breads. When Braidee wanted more food, Lillie Dillie would serve her fresh fruits as fillers. She refused to tell Braidee, "Child, eat as much as you want." Lillie Dillie bought healthy snacks for Braidee and monitored the treats that others served to Braidee. Lillie Dillie created a fun memory with Braidee every time that they made a fruity smoothie together. Braidee enjoyed the cool smoothie spiraling down her throat. This was a great treat that was given to Braidee just before homework began. Braidee would be joyfully humming, slurping her smoothie, and working on math problems. She loved math just as her dad did. Whenever Braidee had math problems that did not make sense, she asked The Bam for help. Whenever she needed to handle a relationship problem, she asked her mother, Lillie Dillie for help. Lillie Dillie was such a nurturing mother. She took care of Braidee and told her that she must brush her teeth two to three times a day so that she would have healthy teeth. Lillie Dillie wished her mother had made her stop eating candy every day.

Intra-Comprehension Questions (ICQ) What happens to teeth that have not been brushed regularly? What happens to the gums?

Lillie Dillie valued chores for Braidee. Lillie Dillie remembered doing small house chores as a little girl. She remembered running errands for the elderly. Hence, Lillie Dillie required that Braidee make her bed daily and empty the trash. Lillie Dillie placed a stool by the kitchen sink so that Braidee could stand on a stool to wash dishes and place them in the dish drain that was on the kitchen counter. Sometimes Braidee would make homemade lemon tea cakes. Lillie Dillie would place the tea cakes in the oven for Braidee. Lillie Dillie would ask measurement questions from the recipes and ask questions relating to the time that the tea cakes had to bake. On the weekend, Braidee would vacuum all the floors in their home. Lillie Dillie did not want Braidee to feel that she was only to clean up her room. Lillie Dillie taught Braidee how to have integrity with these small chores and to serve others. The integrity, Lillie Dillie felt, would carry over to school, college, and marriage life. Integrity would also be needed when Braidee had to live independently, manage her business enterprises, pursue work, choose friends, etc. Braidee did not understand why she had to do things right. She did not know that doing things right would bring her the great rewards of right living and protection. For sure she knew it was wise to honor and obey her parents or else Brady would get hungry for her flesh. Braidee did not like Brady, the belt. Therefore, she made right choices.

Intra-Comprehension Questions (ICQ) What are ways you show your parents that you honor and care for them? Should parents who have made mistakes be forgiven and respected?

Only the right friends and associations could be involved in Braidee's life. Lillie Dillie designed a life for Braidee that was closely monitored. Lillie Dillie only welcomed children who were a good influence on Braidee. Lillie Dillie knew that either Braidee's friends would become like Braidee or Braidee would become like her friends. When school would start, Lillie Dillie would talk to Braidee each day about what happened at school. She would listen carefully for names and influences. Lillie Dillie would invite children over for birthday parties only if they had good character. Lillie Dillie would buy pizza and invite a few of Braidee's friends over for no special occasion, too. Lillie Dillie mainly wanted to hear the conversations and issues that were valued by the children. Sometimes Braidee and her friends would play house and act like mothers. Braidee was the best hair braider and as they played she would braid the hair of the dolls that belonged to her friends. Braidee and her friends were not entertained by the TV. Lillie Dillie had games and craft projects to inspire creativity and develop thinking skills. Occasionally, the children would watch a DVD that influenced them to have good character and make good decisions. The bottom line was that Lillie Dillie wanted to guide all of the children in the right direction.

Lillie Dillie was strict about who Braidee could spend the night with, too. For sure she could spend the weekend with her grandparents and aunts. Lillie Dillie had heard some horror stories about sleep walking uncles, wandering hands, girls experimenting with their bodies, etc. Lillie Dillie protected Braidee from acquiring unnecessary baggage in her life. When Braidee got older, Lillie Dillie did not allow Braidee to chill or hang out like all of the community teens. Braidee felt like she was a square. She felt like she was missing out on all of the fun until some of her classmates got hooked on drugs and became mothers at an early age. She observed how the drug addicts had to support their bad habits and sometimes put their families in danger. The young mothers had to start working instead of starting college. When Braidee saw the big bellies of her classmates and saw classmates high on drugs and spaced out, she thanked her mother for designing a life of success for her. Braidee became more supportive of the concept of "skipping poverty and starting wealthy."Braidee welcomed being groomed to be wealthy!

Intra-Comprehension Questions (ICQ) How many times can you remember when your friends influenced you to do the wrong thing? How many times can you remember when you influenced your friends in the wrong way?

Serving people and money principles were taught as early as Braidee could bring her dad a glass of water and walk and drop a nickel in her piggy bank. A good memory of Lillie Dillie's childhood friend Pudgy, was that his father, Mr. Buckeye, had taught him to save a nickel out of every fifty cents or dollar that he earned. Braidee liked the idea of saving money as a life style. That was so Wow! to Lillie Dillie because she made a lot of mistakes early in life as she wasted her money and misused credit cards. Lillie Dillie said, "never will my children do what I did." Lillie Dillie made sure that Braidee listened to the stories during story time at their public library. She also checked out Big Books and books on tapes and CDs. At home, Lillie Dillie read short books to Braidee that related to building wealth and saving for the future. Before Lillie Dillie began her reading, she asked Braidee to preview the book's front and back cover, pictures or illustrations, captions, contents, and then predict what might possibly happen in the book. After Braidee listened to the story, she shared what part of the book she loved the most. She received blank paper for her to draw in characters and dialogue bubbles of what the characters said in the book. Her pictures and conversations of the characters explained concepts relating to money that she had planned to apply in her life. Braidee gave her mother a brief summary of the main points of her drawings and dialogue.

Lillie Dillie liked how she had served the elderly ladies and was proud of that memory. She passed on that attitude of serving to Braidee. Lillie Dillie and Braidee visited the mother of their church, Ms. Priscilla who was the oldest church member in the congregation and made arrangements for Braidee to help her care for her hair. Braidee always loved braiding hair. Lillie Dillie allowed Braidee to serve Ms. Priscilla and develop her passion of hair braiding simultaneously. Lillie Dillie baked tea cakes and cleaned the kitchen for the mother of the church, too. She washed the dishes and mopped the floor for Ms. Priscilla. Sometimes, she ironed Ms. Priscilla's bloomers for her. Old people liked their underwear ironed back in the old days.

Mr. Buckeye would be so proud of Lillie Dillie for directing Braidee to financial freedom and guiding Braidee slowly to becoming wealthy by working smart, saving consistently, and tying her passion into her career. Lillie Dillie started early guiding Braidee in the right financial direction. Lillie Dillie accompanied Braidee to meetings with free financial advisors at the credit union in order for her to learn about the operating the rule of 72, accumulating compound interest over 20 to 30 + years, Roth IRAs, etc. Lillie Dillie wanted Braidee to value saving money early in life. Lillie Dillie groomed Braidee from childhood to become wealthy. Lillie

Dillie had plans to turn the hair braiding into another stream of wealth. The Bam and Lillie Dillie were planning to help Braidee establish her very on braiding hair business. Braidee started saving part of her allowance for her business, too.

Great parents support passion and entrepreneurship as The Bam and Lillie Dillie did. Braidee had parent support and a passion for hair braiding starting from her childhood, through high school and college. This cultivating of Braidee's passion helped Braidee to be a master stylist. When Braidee became a senior in high school, she had a great desire to serve a cause greater than her. She started a Senior's Groom To Be Wealthy Club. All members of the club had to have aspirations to combine their passion with their business, save money, and operate a budget no matter how much money they had. If parents had to be guardians of checking and savings accounts, that is what had to happen. As President of the club, she invited a variety of speakers to volunteer and speak about how to start up a business, business insurance, life insurance, medical and dental insurance, monthly systematic mutual fund accounts, accelerated payments on mortgage loans. Some speakers educated seniors about alternatives to health insurances for the self-employed who did not have the benefits of group insurance. Some speakers spoke about wills and trusts. Some volunteers became mentors to the seniors who were interested in real estate, cash management accounts, franchises, and purchases of gold. Some mentors helped the students develop business plans and marketing strategies. The senior class of Linear High School especially loved to learn about practical strategies to save money and build wealth by Mrs. J of Xcellent Info Publishing. Braidee also met with several corporate sponsors in order to ask for scholarship funds to help the less fortunate seniors to attend college. She had been saving since she was two years old and her parents had been saving to help her skip poverty and start wealthy. College funds were not a problem for Braidee. Braidee and all of the seniors went to the college of their choice for 4 years.

Intra-Comprehension Questions (ICQ) How are you going to tie in your passion with your college career? What is your action plan?

Resources had always been provided to Braidee. Lillie Dillie loved to research and collect knowledge and resources that she shared with whoever would listen. Braidee, in her elementary years and high school years, had to complete her teachers' assignments plus her mother's home assignments and do chores. When the technology age began, Braidee had to use online encyclopedias and online dictionaries. (www.webster-dictionary.net, www.Merriam-webster.com, and www.worldbookonline.com) Oh, as for character development, character education was always modeled and valued in Braidee's home. And Lillie Dillie was known for asking Braidee's friends, "How is your character? Are you saving for your future?" Lillie Dillie would use the Internet to give Braidee and her friends practice in recording fake transactions on the Daily Tracking Practice web page on www.MultiplicationShake.com. Later, she would give them an Xcellent Checkbook Registry to manually track their money. Lillie Dillie loved helping everyone!

The Bam and Lillie Dillie rewarded Braidee for all of her years of hard work. When Braidee was in high school, her parents awarded her "private living quarters" because she made straight A's in most of her classes and had perfect attendance at school and perfect attendance where she worked. She worked in the local salon shampooing hair and braiding hair for the community's expert cosmetologists. She had to budget the money that she made. Briefly speaking, she had to tithe, save, and invest at least $25 a month in a systematic investment account. She also had to buy gas for her used car, and buy hair supplies for her hair clients. She had to use the Internet to get a big picture of how to budget. (www.MultiplicationShake.com) Braidee managed her money as a kid. As she became older, she set up her budget. It was expected that she would set up a budget before she made her first pay check in college. Of course, a business budget would be expected in her future business operations. We are really going to describe Braidee's "private living quarters" so get ready to "dream." Her parents made this grand investment so that Braidee could live at home after college until she learned more about life and living independently. The remodeling company had several options for the family to choose from. They put their ideas together and put together combinations of plans. This is the result.

Braidee's "private living quarters" was secured with a locking door that lead to her parent's upstairs living area. Braidee's parents agreed to respect Braidee's privacy because they trusted her and believed that she would make good decisions about the who, what, and when of her mini apartment. Braidee had a private driveway and a silent garage to the entrance of her living quarters. Braidee lived in a large basement that was divided into an entertainment room, bedroom, bathroom kitchen, and laundry room. The entertainment room had a big screen television with a theatre sound system, DVD player, lap top computer, and a wall-to-wall sofa as well as a wall-to-wall book shelf. Braidee's fireplace was installed between her bedroom and entertainment room. It was cozy! In addition to the fireplace, Braidee's bedroom was large enough for a study desk and chair with bright lighting for study time. Braidee had a Jacuzzi®, separate shower, and two entrance doors so that her guests could enter the bathroom without entering her bedroom. Braidee's bedroom closet, bathroom closet, kitchen pantry, and laundry room were all professionally shelved because Braidee valued order and cleanliness. There was a fully equipped quaint kitchen that had a commercial blender especially used to prepare lots of fruity smoothies.

Intra-Comprehension Questions (ICQ) Do you think that Braidee's hard work should be awarded? Explain. Are you be responsible enough to live in an independent living quarters as Braidee did? Explain.

Braidee's College Life

Braidee completed her high school credits four months before her graduation date. Braidee was smart for her age. She included that statement in a poem that she wrote when she was in preschool. The poem was published in the newspaper and read by every citizen in Baker, Louisiana. It was a big deal to have a poem placed in the newspaper. Lillie Dillie taught Braidee academic lessons after Braidee completed her homework all through Braidee's elementary school years. Their hard work paid off and one of the rewards was an early high school graduation. Because Braidee had finished meeting her graduation requirements, she had time to check the status of her college application. She also had time to search for scholarship funds and college loans for other students because her father had saved up money for Braidee's college expenses. Braidee also had time to go prepare for college entrance tests and visit several colleges. She chose two Historically Black Colleges as her top choices. They were Grambling State University and Southern University. Visiting the library was one of Braidee's favorite pastimes. She would ask the librarian to show her the Occupation Outlook Handbook and then she would research the skills and the salaries for her industry. She would also skim through the college planning search materials. Braidee accessed a lot of college websites in the library. She was most impressed when she saw ways to save money while in college, such as buying used books instead of new books. Braidee had study notes that she knew she would need in college. She organized her study notes and test taking strategies. She packed her best examples of research papers. Braidee had planned to get a part-time job while in college, like her mother did. She packed sample cover letters and resumes. She was so organized. She made a folder in her laptop of the electronic research resources that will make her research thorough. Braidee had a checklist to check off what she needed to pack. And of course, she had to talk to her dear old grandmother before leaving for college. She could count on her saying, "keep your mind on books and not boys."

Braidee told Mama Isabelle, her dad's mother, about her plans to go away to school. Mama Isabelle told her to get a good education, and get her future together before she even thinks about marriage. She advised Braidee to remember her raising, and not to go the way of the world when she got to college. She told Braidee to take her bible, inspirational DVDS, and family memoirs to school with her. She also gave Braidee a lecture on Do's and Don'ts in college. Mama Isabelle's Do list included:

1) Do go to church and keep your creator in your life. Do not go wild, child.
2) Do be happy and thankful you did well in classes in middle school and high school so now you don't have to take remedial classes in college. You will not have to pay for classes that do not count toward your degree. That saves you money.
3) Do get your education because you will have a hard time in life without an education. Do have a plan for handling conflicts with teachers and students.
4) Do stay on campus and stay away from wild parties. She told Braidee stories about the Spanish Fly. She said if it is placed in your drink, you will lose your mind. Watch your soft drinks, Braidee.
5) Do set up a study schedule and live by it. Turn off the TV all week long.
6) Do choose a good roommate. Choose someone who will respect your need to study.
7) Do talk to your instructors and ask for help. They are there to help you.
8) Do get a part-time job and start saving money for the future. If you don't die, you will live and need money to have a good life.
9) Do drop college classes that you are flunking immediately and take them at a later date. Get a tutor.

Mama Isabelle's Don'ts list included:

1) Don't forget your upbringing. Certain things you were not raised to do.
2) Don't waste study time watching TV and hanging out in the student union. Retaking classes gets expensive.
3) Don't get pregnant. Your whole life will be taken from you. You will have to give up your education and go to work.
4) Don't stay out partying all night and sleep through classes.
5) Don't smoke marijuana to feel good. It will lead you to wanting a greater high with cocaine. Once you are hooked, you life is doomed and you will be destined to failure.
6) Don't run up any credit card debt. Bad debt is like a noose around your neck. It is easy to get on and difficult to pay off. Bad debt takes years to pay off.
7) Don't sit on the walls watching guys pass by and miss classes.

8) Don't get a degree in something easy just to say you graduated. Get a degree in a field that is related to your "passion". Love what you do for a living and you will love getting paid for having fun.

Braidee took heed to what Mama Isabelle said just as she took heed to what Pastor Randy, the youth pastor at her church, said to all of the graduates. At church Braidee and all of the graduates, were recognized by the youth pastor. The graduates were called to the stage and given a bible and applause. Pastor Randy prayed that each graduate would go forward in the world, do great things, and leave a legacy. Pastor Randy preached sermons that influenced Braidee to put the Almighty first, go to college and come back and become the greatest business woman ever. Braidee loved Pastor Randy and had plans to fly back home to attend the Empowerment Conferences every first week of May.

Intra-Comprehension Questions (ICQ) What does taking "heed" mean? What are some negative consequences when you don't take heed?

After Braidee had listened to her grandmother and her pastor, she prepared to attend her number one choice of college, Grambling State University which was in Grambling, Louisiana. Braidee was driven to college by her parents. Braidee cried when she first arrived to Grambling State University because she knew that she would really miss her family. Braidee's high school friends attended Grambling State University with her. Taking a walk with her friends helped her to stop crying. She and her friends walked to the cafeteria together every evening together. A typical meal might consist of a green salad, a hamburger, dessert, milk and juice. Once the girls settled in and all the crying ceased, Braidee had to remember that Mama Isabelle had said, "Don't sit on the wall, watch guys, and miss classes. Even thou Mama Isabelle's advice had followed Braidee all the way to Grambling State University, she still watched all the cute guys in the cafeteria.

Mama Isabelle had not said a thing about the street dances or the Friday movies. Braidee and her friends spent late hours dancing at the street dances and watching the boys. On Fridays, Braidee and her friends went to the movies and sat in the balcony of the Grambling State University auditorium. Again, they were watching boys. On Saturdays Braidee hosted a Study Hardy Party. She and the Student Government President led students in setting up their outlines for math assignments and math projects. The study groups were divided so as to make sure that a strong math student and a strong researcher was in each group. The role of the strong math student was to keep everyone abreast of rudimentary math concepts. The role of the researcher was to keep a math dictionary and a resourceful math website available. When everyone understood his or her part and was on a roll, Braidee played upbeat instrumental music. They were bobbing heads and tapping feet as they worked on their projects. Brain foods such as bran muffins, fruits, and pancakes were available for snacks. Each group held their members accountable for really studying, attending class and graduating with honors. On Monday morning, Braidee arrived to class on time. She organized her binders by colors. She had bought all of her books for math class. She had no trouble with any of the math classes. The Bam, her father, was a math major at Grambling State University. Braidee worked in the math department through a work study program. She offered tutoring sessions to struggling students. After each pay period, Braidee paid her tithes and saved her money for the purpose of marketing her business in the future.

Braidee's friend, Lori, worked to pay for her college expenses. Lori didn't have parents who had saved for her college expenses. Lori did receive Vocational Rehabilitation assistance to help pay for college and book expenses.

Braidee's college classes were spread out. She went to three classes on Mondays, three classes on Wednesdays, and three classes on Fridays. She worked part-time and studied on Tuesdays, Thursdays, Saturdays and Sundays. Braidee used her research skills and note-taking skills extensively in order to maintain her honors status. Braidee made side line money braiding the hair of many students. She used the money to buy quality products to satisfy her customers. She intentionally wanted to satisfy her current customers in order to gain more customers. She understood the power of "word of mouth" advertising. As she took business classes, she learned the procedures to legally set up a braiding salon and rent out booths. She inquired about business taxes, too.

Intra-Comprehension Questions (ICQ) How should Braidee handle clients who want to pay on credit? Should Braidee set up a legal entity in college?

Braidee deals with adversity just as she was taught to in her childhood. Braidee was an entrepreneur in the making in college. There were a few students who were jealous about how beautifully she could braid hair. However, she made friends with a new freshman named Debra. Braidee could handle associates making jealous remarks. She did not need to call home for help with such a minute problem. Braidee made quite a bit of money braiding hair in college. Braidee and Debra walked to the cafeteria each evening and looked at everybody who was sitting on the walls watching everybody walk by. Debra's hair was beautifully braided. Braidee had placed shiny hair decorations in Debra's braids. Braidee and Debra did not stay on the same floor at Grambling State University in Wheatley Hall. However, the girls would meet in the lobby and go to class or to the cafeteria. They would wait on Lori, too. They could count on the older guys at Grambling State University to always find time to come watch the freshman girls walk in and out of the dormitory. The girls were also guilty of being excited about boy watching.

The first two days she was at college, Braidee had a room all alone. She had a small refrigerator, a hot plate, a few plates, silverware, and two black skillets. Remember she liked everything in place. When she became hungry late at night, Braidee fried french fries. Therefore, eating late at night solved her hunger problems until her next meal, breakfast, would be served. To Braidee's surprise, her roommate arrived from New York early one Saturday morning. She brought in a stereo, gigantic speakers, and wall-to-wall CDs. Her roommate had a noisy, loud family, too. Braidee could see that this was going to be a long semester with all that noise.

Arva was the name of Braidee's roommate. Arva brought her whole family and a 22 inch flat screen television. Braidee's eyes and head bucked. She could not believe all of the noise and drama that that family brought into their dormitory room. She did not like noise. Therefore, after the introductions, she smiled and told everyone that it was nice to meet them. She walked to a private area and called her mother and told her every detail. She exaggerated a bit, too. Her mother, Lillie Dillie, asked her, "What are you going to do, Braidee?" Braidee replied, "I am going to talk to Daddy. He will know just what I can do to take care of this problem." He is a cool dad.

Intra-Comprehension Questions (ICQ) What do you think her Dad will advise her to do? Do you think that she will do exactly what he advises? Explain.

Braidee hung up the phone and rode the elevator up to Debra's room. Debra was nowhere to be found. Lori was nowhere in sight either. Braidee felt like running back home. Then she remembered how she was raised to not quit hard things. She was taught to quit things that were not right for her. She had been taught to talk things out to solve problems. She was taught to "think" out a strategy to deal with problems tactfully. Her dad had read a book called How to Deal with Problems Tactfully. She recalled a discussion that The Bam had with her after he had finished reading the book. She took a deep breath and thought about every step that she would take.

Can you guess her next step?

Braidee visualized herself walking back into the dormitory. Braidee visualized a script. She loved to plan out her strategies. Most folks think of the wrong answer immediately. Braidee knew breaking up the CDs would start a fight. She knew snatching the plug out of the wall while the CDs were playing would provoke Arva to lash out. She knew screaming and using profanity was not her character and those behaviors would create an immediate enemy. So Braidee thought about how she would want to be approached. She knew that "talking" was what would work for her. She didn't know Arva. However, she knew that a right attitude, right body language, and right voice tones work with any stranger. After having thought this out, Braidee wrote out her script. She practiced soft inflections, too. She wanted to talk to her roommate without a. She sometimes preferred to have a mediator who would begin the mediation with the question, "What was happening when?" and end with "How do we move forward positively?". The oral script would sound somewhat like this:

Braidee: Hey Arva. Your folks were really nice.

Arva: Yeah, I think so, too. Thank you for that nice compliment.

Braidee: I can't wait for you to meet my parents. My mother is going to ask you, "How is your character?" So, don't be offended. Momma will tell you to get an education and get your future together. My Auntie will tell you, "Right is right. It is nice to be nice."

Arva: What cool peeps! My dear old grandma passed last year. I miss eating her tea cakes.

Braidee: Arva, new subject. I liked that song that you were blasting when I was on the way out of the door earlier this morning.

Arva: Yeah, that was "Dawn of A New Day" by Ava and Noelle. Sister girl, you can buy it on CDBaby.com. That song has gotten me through a lot of hard times.

Braidee: Cool! I'll do that. Arva, the other thing I really, really want to talk about is not the name of the song. I have another concern. In my family, we talked about our concerns before they became big problems.

Arva: Well, in my family we shoot straight to the hip. Braidee, what's the deal?

Braidee: Arva, we just met and I don't want to sound like a negative complainer.

Arva: Then don't. Talk from your heart. I won't get mad.

Braidee: OK. OK. I loved "Dawn of A New Day." We are beginning our new life in college. It's a dawn of a new commencement of adulthood.

Arva: Braidee, you are sweating me out! Talk girl!

Braidee: OK. OK. Forgive me for being so gentle with you.

Arva: Spare me. Go ahead.

Braidee: Arva, the volume of your music is my concern. I want us to be good roomies who know each after our college days are over. Let's set some ground rules for how we will live as successful roomies.

Arva: I like that. I'll set ground rule number one. The first rule is to talk without procrastinating. Tell me what is on your mind first. Please, don't go up and down the hallways in the dormitory gossiping about my music.

Braidee: OK. Rule number two. We'll turn our music down so that our neighbors in the dormitory won't report our loud music to the house mother or the RA (Resident Assistant). And I need a quiet environment.

Arva: Braidee, look. Stop worrying already. I have earphones. I wear them. On the day everybody was here, we jammed. During study hours, I know to wear my earphones. Check them out.

Braidee: Oh, these are nice. Moving on to rule number three. Ask before borrowing each other's belongings. And no lending to anyone who does not live in our room, not even a tiny bit of shampoo.

Arva: That works for me. Rule number four is being polite. Stay quiet when the other person is sleeping.

Braidee: OK. Here is a biggie. Rule number five is related to morals. No sneaking boys in our room.

Arva: Don't go there, Braidee. You don't know me that well.

Braidee: This must be a good place to stop. I am going to take a shower and get ready to walk to the cafeteria. I'll meet Debra and Lori, my friends in the lobby. We'll be happy to have you join us.

Intra-Comprehension Questions (ICQ) What is a good rule for when one of the roommates leaves the room to take a shower? Explain.

Braidee and Arva got along quite well. Braidee bought discipline to college. She would read 3 or 4 chapters per night. She would outline the chapters. She felt that the reading was benefitting her. Therefore, she did not depend on her professors to make her read. Braidee tutored some of the students who had failed math and other orientation classes. Some of them kept on partying. Their punishment was that their parents had to pay for classes that they were failing. This was hurtful for their entire family. Ouch.

Braidee wanted to work in The Collegiate Shoppe just as her mother had when she was at Grambling State University. She prepared herself for her interview. She dared not to chew gum. She could hear her mother saying, "Chew gum at home and not in the public." So you know she couldn't chew gum in an interview. Braidee practiced answering some questions that she thought she would be asked. She was prepared to share how much her mother loved working at the fashion store. Excellent work ethics were modeled for Braidee. Her mother, Lillie Dillie, had worked as a Residential Assistant at Southern University in Baton Rouge, LA. Her dad, The Bam, worked at Dow Chemical for 18 years and was not absent one day. Braidee felt like it was an honor to follow such great role models. She knew her mother's history of wasting money. However, she surely forgave her and her appreciate the great model she was in work ethics. Braidee dressed appropriately for the interview. She knew that the Collegiate Shoppe was a classy store. She dressed in a nice navy business suit with a nice pair of closed in shoes with a heel not too high. She reached her hand out and gave a firm handshake and a beautiful smile. She had researched the company and read current news articles about this high fashion clothing shop. She knew the mission statement, the vision, and the owners so well. Remember, her mother Lillie Dillie Richardson had worked for Mr. Wilkerson, the original owner of the Collegiate Shoppe. She answered each question better than she had rehearsed. Braidee was hired. She was ten minutes early on her first day of work. She vacuumed, dusted, and waited on customers. Before she got her pay check, she wrote out her budget and saved nearly seventy percent of her money. She had planned to use the money for the down payment to purchase of her Braiding Salon. It seemed that the years passed by so quickly. Braidee loved completing her business projects and assignments and helping others. She loved hosting the Study Hardy Parties on Saturday mornings. She also loved the street dances and the Friday night movies. These were things that her parents had done when they were college sweethearts. She wanted to be able to compare the music and the styles of dances with her parents.

Braidee had conquered her task of graduating from Grambling State University. She sent out her invitations and all of the Johnsons and Richardsons were there. Trunk loads of food were brought to Grambling, Louisiana. She had sweet potatoes pies from all of the grandmothers in the family. She requested several kinds of chicken like honey lemon and Southern fried chicken. Debra was asking about collard greens and turkey necks with hot water cornbread, too. Braidee asked her family to set up everything in a banquet room in the union across from the cafeteria. She invited staff from the Collegiate Shoppe, former Professors, and friends who lived in her dormitory. Of course, Arva had to attend. She wanted to blast her music. Braidee gave her a look that said, "Not on my special day." As this glorious day came to an end, Braidee had to load all of her possessions in a trailer. The Bam and The Power Team, the young guys in our family, took only forty-five minutes to load each box into the trailer. Braidee thanked everyone for coming, thanked them for the gifts, and gave everybody a grateful hug. She was excited about her new life. The Bam, her dad, gave her access to the investment that he had made for her all of the years that she attended college. He had rented out the mini-apartment that was attached to their home. He invested that rental fee in risky stock investments because he understood how investments work. Braidee had also earned quite a stash of money when she worked off campus. Braidee had been influenced to be a professional business woman. The speakers who used to volunteer their time to speak at the Groom To Be Wealthy educational seminars were so proud of Braidee. Braidee had written her business plan and marketing plan in her business class in Grambling. With all of this combined knowledge, she and her father visited a real estate company in her home town. They discussed buying a business suite that was in foreclosure. The real estate agent made a fair deal. He also connected them with a banker who was excited about selling the foreclosed property. Braidee would embrace a win-win situation. The Bam and Braidee subcontracted out jobs and renovated the building. Braidee was the owner of Braidee's Braiding Salon. She rented out booths to self-employed hair stylists, manicurist, and massage therapist. A portion of her building had child care for their clients and staff. There was a healthy food's café in the business suite, too. One of Braidee's friends had studied agriculture. He owned a farm and provided all fresh vegetables that were sold in the café. Braidee loved her staff who were also her former elementary and high school friends. They all planned to become entrepreneurs who would rent from Braidee after they all graduated from various colleges. Braidee rented yachts and planned family trips for her occupants. They felt loved and were productive. They were walking advertisers for Braidee's Hair Salon because she cared about their well-being as well as their family's well-being. As promised, they took turns going back into the local schools to conduct volunteer Groom To Be Wealthy educational seminars. Mrs. Johnson was more passionate than ever about teaching early money management skills to everyone. She was still insisting that kids practice plugging in checking and savings transactions on her Daily Tracking Practice on www.MultiplicationShake.com. Others were still sending kids to the website, too. The kids were excited about printing out their transactions and showing them to their moms. We had plans for every generation of our families to groom to be wealthy. Braidee and her friends had vowed that they were the generation where the alcoholic, the women chaser, and money waster curses were stopping. To this day, their generational wealth is still passing from one generation to another, intentionally. They don't engage in former generational curses.

Intra-Comprehension Questions (ICQ) Are you aware of the generational wealth in your family? Are you choosing to be the first one to build generational wealth rather than generational curses? Are you even planning to be the first college graduate of your family?

It was no doubt that these young entrepreneurs were going to be successful. Braidee invited a marketing speaker to come speak to the graduates. They were excited about their first meeting after graduation. Braidee was still a leading force in getting the best speakers ever to speak to the Groom To Be Wealthy Club. Braidee strongly encouraged all participants to bring laptops. When the speaker walked in, we could see her brand. She wore colors that matched intentionally. Her brochure matched her outfit. And we looked out of the window, and saw that her car matched her fashionable clothes, too. The speaker came in and talked about several topics. She talked about how to brand a business. Branding was not difficult for us because we were all trained in a career that is also our passion. So we could brand our businesses after seeing the speaker, Mrs. Sharpe. Mrs. Sharpe guided us in how to write down clear vision and mission statements. She guided us in writing down our target market or the people we want to sell our services and products to, too. She had demonstrated how to use technology to reach the neighborhood clients. Patiently, we engaged in hands-on experiences. Some graduates wanted to reach the international sector. That was no big deal for Mrs. Sharpe. One person asked how, "How would I hire a marketing consultant?" Mrs. Sharpe recommended that the person must have good character and integrity. Whether you search the Internet or the yellow pages, the marketer must be of character and knowledgeable. She said that you don't want to deal with a marketer who won't return your phone calls. This would be evidence that the person will not return the calls of your prospects. Mrs. Sharpe felt that communicating with three references of the interviewee would be wise. She said "work for hire" contracts would keep each party involved aware of his or her expectations. Negotiate a price that is comfortable for both of you. You want to pay for massive exposure. Mrs. Sharpe gave each entrepreneur a sheet of paper. Each was challenged to create a draft of the most unique logo, business card, brochure and flier. Mrs. Sharpe demonstrated the wrong way and the correct way to make an introductory call. Next, each student had to had to demonstrate how to successfully make introductory calls. Mrs. Sharpe ended with instruction and demonstration on how to build databases and send massive emails. She said,

> Market, market, market, and keep marketing. Ask everybody you meet what they have a need for. Then share with them how the features and the benefits of your services and products fit their needs. Attend as many networking events as you are able, too. As you share your business card, be excited about what you have to contribute to make the world a better place. Your potential clients will want to be a part of your something good.

Braidee had a big picture of how to market her Braiding Salon. She was ready to move forward in entrepreneurship. Braidee's parents had given her the money that they had collected for rent. Braidee's parents also had given her a life-impacting graduation gift which was cosigning for a business loan and making sure that Braidee's name was on the mortgage for the ownership of the building. Placing Braidee's name on the contract would help Braidee to build good credit in her name. This would also make Braidee the owner of a building that contained her salon which will be called Braidee's Salon. The paper work was set up with Braidee's name included with the intention of Braidee being the sole owner of her salon and sole payer of the loan in a year or sooner. Braidee decorated her salon immaculately and rented out booths to experts who would provide services as massagers, manicurists, and pedicurists. Braided valued the relationships that she had built in high school and was excited about the possibility of all of her friends building wealth along with her. You can guess that Braidee braided hair for hours and made a fortune doing what she loved to do. The integrity that she developed in childhood was manifested in her business dealings. The fruity smoothies, healthy sandwiches, and tea cakes that she loved as a child were served in the Braidee's Healthy Café which was conveniently located in her salon. Braidee paid students who were members of the Groom To Be Wealthy Club to work in her café so that they could gain experience in extending quality service to people, developing character, and assisting in running a successful business. Braidee kept the legacy of helping lower economic seniors attend college and promised that they could always work for her. She passed on the concept of "skipping poverty and starting wealthy" to every student, client, and self-employed occupant in her salon. Braidee showed relational wealth in a big way by helping others reach their destiny and caring about the development of others. She supported helping them to develop to their fullest potential.

You may remember that Mr. Buckeye wanted the students in the classrooms that he presented to develop to their fullest potential, too. Braidee invited him to speak to her staff. Since Braidee owned the shop and the self-employed staff had a need to understand keeping good records, Mr. Buckeye taught them all some very basic record-keeping tips. He advised them to type in a Word document, manually record information in a record keeping book, or buy special software. Whatever tool is used, people need to place the dates, track the amount of or quantity of supplies ordered and the costs. Include contact information or (if using a book), attach a business card so that it will be easy to contact the company for more supplies. Keep a close eye on your inventory and keep supplies ready. On the sales record sheets, write the dates, track the items, the costs of the items, and the totals of the sales. On the services sheets, type in the dates, the services rendered to others, and the cost of the services. This information will help you complete the income statement, which is sometimes called the profit and loss (income) statement. It is imperative to record the totals of income or revenue, the costs of goods sold, and the profit of sales in the income statement. The operation expenses and the losses need to be recorded in the income statement regularly. The cash flow statement will contain cash balances, cash received, cash paid out for goods and services, different expenses, and ending cash balances. A basic business balance sheet contains assets (what you own), liabilities (what you owe), and net worth. Net worth is the difference between assets and liabilities. Mr. Buckeye advised the staff to hire an expert who is called a certified tax accountant. This expert will guide you in organizing the income from sales and organizing expenses such as rental expenses and supplies. For a monthly fee, he or she will do all of the work for you. Mr. Buckeye strongly advised the staff to always make sure that there is more income than expenses or expenditures. He informed the young entrepreneurs to file folders in a portable carrier or a file cabinet. Accounts receivables represents money owed you by people who buy your sales items or services. Accounts payables represent money you owe people for their services and products. Both accounts receivables and the account payables may be filed in ABC order. Taxes, social security, medical insurance, and dental insurance are deducted from the salaries of legal business owners and employees as well as self-employed business owners. Be prepared to pay your ongoing partner, the government. Income taxes need to be saved for in the event one has to pay back the government. This business of record keeping can become very complex. It is better to plan to pay someone to help you than to have to pay the government or Uncle Sam an abundance of money. Browse www.nolo.com and www.ask.com and search bookkeeping for professional bookkeeping advice. Samples of balance sheets may be available.

Compound Interest & The Rule of 72

Take the time to empower yourself to be an excellent record keeper. Take time to find out the details of how compound interest can earn you interest on interest. Take time to use a simple formula – The Rule of 72 – to find out how many years it will take your money to double. Can you divide 72 by 9? This is how easy it is to find out how many years it will take your money to double. Your money is expected to double in 8 years, depending on the economy. And finally, take time to seek professional advice about the meaning of any financial concept that you have read about.

Teaching Aids Section

This section contains a wide variety of worksheets, projects, tools, and songs designed to be used to reinforce ideas and information about money management and related subjects.

Schedules for Structuring Discipline

Daily schedules help us live life by design and not from crisis to crisis. In the schedules, include homework, talent development, light chores, and spiritual development.

Make extra copies before you write on this copy. Use a new copy weekly or as the schedule changes.

Name _____ Date _____

MONDAY - Daily After School Schedule

3:00 PM – I will _____

4:00 PM – I will _____

5:00 PM – I will _____

6:00 PM – I will _____

7:00 PM – I will _____

8:00 PM – I will _____

9:00 PM – I will _____

10:00 PM – I will _____

Name _____ Date _____

TUESDAY - Daily After School Schedule

3:00 PM – I will _____

4:00 PM – I will _____

5:00 PM – I will _____

6:00 PM – I will _____

7:00 PM – I will _____

8:00 PM – I will _____

9:00 PM – I will _____

10:00 PM – I will _____

Name _____ Date _____

WEDNESDAY - Daily After School Schedule

3:00 PM – I will _____

4:00 PM – I will _____

5:00 PM – I will _____

6:00 PM – I will _____

7:00 PM – I will _____

8:00 PM – I will _____

9:00 PM – I will _____

10:00 PM – I will _____

Name _____ Date _____

THURSDAY - Daily After School Schedule

3:00 PM – I will _____

4:00 PM – I will _____

5:00 PM – I will _____

6:00 PM – I will _____

7:00 PM – I will _____

8:00 PM – I will _____

9:00 PM – I will _____

10:00 PM – I will _____

Name _____ Date _____

FRIDAY - Daily After School Schedule

3:00 PM – I will _____

4:00 PM – I will _____

5:00 PM – I will _____

6:00 PM – I will _____

7:00 PM – I will _____

8:00 PM – I will _____

9:00 PM – I will _____

10:00 PM – I will _____

Name _____ Date_____

SATURDAY - Weekend Schedule

Arise early and complete chores. Chores develop discipline and character. Enjoy family time.

8:00 AM – I will _____

9:00 AM – I will _____

10:00 AM – I will _____

11:00 AM – I will _____

12:00 PM – Rest of Day – Our family will _____

8:00 PM – I will _____

9:00 PM – I will _____

10:00 PM – I will _____

Name _____ Date_____

SUNDAY – Weekend Schedule

Arise early and enjoy family worship. Spiritual development fulfills a void that man can't.

8:00 AM – I will _____

9:00 AM – I will _____

10:00 AM – I will _____

11:00 AM – Our family will _____

12:00 PM – Rest of Day – Our family will _____

8:00 PM – I will _____

9:00 PM – I will _____

10:00 PM – I will _____

Money Management

Money Management Terms and Musical Chairs

Directions: Use these words as vocabulary words and spelling words. Assign the words in sets or all of them at one time. Consider the levels of the students. Students may begin the activities by ABC ordering the words, then defining them, writing sentences, stories, raps, poems, songs, etcetera with them. Be creative with word puzzles and games. Provide online websites such as www.Merriam-Webster.com, www.Webster-Dictionary.net, www.MathIsFun.com, and www.BusinessDictionary.com.

Increase the memory of vocabulary and spellings with our music, "The Multiplication Shake" CD and musical chairs. Music integrated with academics increases achievement infinitely. Check out our link on www.MultiplicationShake.com.

1. compound interest

2. rule of 72

3. budget

4. high debt to low income

5. inventory

6. percent

7. decimal

8. tithe

9. fraction

10. track manually

11. diversify

12. balance

13. checkbook

14. outstanding checks

15. investment

16. net worth

17. income

18. expenditures

19. interest rate

20. utility bills

21. manager

22. safe deposit box

23. surplus budget

24. taxes

25. save

26. real estate

27. fixed assets

28. fixed expenses

29. garnish

30. mortgage

31. discipline

32. ACH

33. financial statement

34. online banking

35. debit card

36. credit card

37. rent

38. wealth

39. ATM

40. Deposit

41. withdrawal

42. vault

43. interest

44. allowance

45. debt

46. cash flow

47. financial goals

Answer Key for Money Management Terms

Directions: Use these words as vocabulary words and spelling words. Assign the words in sets or all of them at one time. Consider the levels of the students. Students may begin the activities by ABC ordering the words, then defining them, writing sentences, stories, raps, poems, songs, etcetera with them. Be creative. Provide online websites such as www.Merriam-Webster.com, www.Webster-Dictionary.net, www.MathIsFun.com, and www.BusinessDictionary.com.

Increase the memory of vocabulary and spellings with our music CD, "The Multiplication Shake" and musical chairs. Music integrated with academics increases retention and achievement infinitely.

1. compound interest – interest earned on interest

2. rule of 72 – the time it takes for invested money to double; divide the 72 by the percentage rate. Example: the percentage rate is 8 percent, 72 ÷ 8 = 9. It can be projected that it will take 9 years for the money to double in value.

3. budget – a plan that guides the manager in the best way to save and spend money; handle by making good money decisions

4. high debt to low income – having more debt to repay to creditors or lenders than money earned; prevents important purchases such as homes, cars, etc.

5. inventory – record of goods on hand; a list of goods

6. percent – based on the number 100

7. decimal – based on the number 10

8. tithe – tenth of earnings freely given to support the church

9. fraction – part of a whole

10. track manually – keep good records of money by handwriting; not the internet

11. diversify – place money in several places such as stocks, bonds, mutual funds, etc.

12. balance – what is left; balance a checkbook by keeping equality or a record of what is available to spend and what is actually spent

13. checkbook – register to record money transactions

14. outstanding checks – checks that have not been paid or deducted from your checking account; keep money in the account for the checks that still need to be paid

15. investment – money placed in accounts with the intent of growing and making money for the future; property acquired to appreciate or grow in value

16. net worth – is the sum of the issued share capital, retained earnings, and capital gain; what one owns or assets; value of a firm to its owners

17. income – money earned for work rendered; salary

18. expenditures – same as expenses; bills; disbursements that are paid; payments

19. interest rate – when investing, the interest rate is paid to you when a larger firm lends out your money that they borrow form you ; when borrowing, it is a fee paid to the creditor or lender for borrowing their money; annual cost of credit

20. utility bills – payments to companies for using their services such as electric, gas, water, etc.

21. manager – caretaker of money; one who makes wise decisions with money

22. safe deposit box – box to store very important papers and other valuable collections

23. surplus budget – a plan for handling money that has extra money; have more than the amount of money needed to pay disbursements or bills

24. taxes – fees paid to the government on products, incomes, or business earnings

25. save – put away for the future; store money for future usage

26. real estate – land, home, property that appreciates or becomes valuable

27. fixed assets – assets generate profits and the profits are expected to last or be in use for more than one year such as land, buildings, machinery, etc.

28. fixed expenses – expenses are taken from earnings and are expected to last or be paid out for more than one year such as mortgages, car notes, insurance, etc.

29. garnish – take money from your paycheck in part or in full by court order for taxes owed or debts owed; legal summons to stop wages or garnishment

30. mortgage – contract for the purchase of home; payments made to a lender with the expectation of ownership

31. discipline – control of emotions and habits; regulation of habits; work on a schedule; learn to control actions through self-motivation, punishment, or as a result of being taught; an area of study (financial literacy)

32. ACH – Automated Clearing House – automatic withdrawal from a checking or savings account to pay a creditor

33. financial statement – a statement that list the current balance and the previous transactions in checking and savings accounts

34. online banking – using the internet to check balances and deposits related to your financial accounts (checking, savings, and much more)

35. debit card – purchase goods with plastic card; use your money that is available in your checking account

36. credit card – purchase goods with a plastic card; a loan; pay back amount borrowed plus interest (additional money)

37. rent – monthly payment to live in a property with no ownership intentions

38. wealth – upward mobility; abundance; lots of possessions or things; riches; affluence

39. ATM – Automated Teller Machine – can quickly withdraw cash from your bank account using ATM

40. deposit – to place money in an account; add the amount to your balance in your checking or savings account balance

41. withdrawal – to take money out of an account; subtract the amount from your checking or savings account balance

42. vault – keep money safe secure room with thick walls to a heavy steel door

43. interest – banks borrow money from savings accounts and pay account holders interest or money

44. allowance – money earned after a job has been properly completed

45. debt – money owed to a creditor or lender; paid back with interest fees

46. cash flow – incomings and outgoings of cash; the difference between an opening balance and a closing balance

47. financial goals – plans or intentions for money; goals must be specific, measurable, observable, and achieved by a certain time period

Samples of Interests and the Rule of 72

Simple Interest

Simple interest is the interest paid on the savings deposit.

For Example:

$600 x 0.06 = $36.00

Year 1

Compound Interest

Compound interest is the interest paid on the savings deposit plus interest paid annually or quarterly. The $36 was added to the $600. Then we multiplied by the interest of 6%.

For Example:

$636 x 0.06 = $38.16

$636 + $38.16 = $674.16

The Rule of 72

The Rule of 72 is the time it takes for money in a savings or investments account to "double".

For Example:

If your savings account earns 8% percent interest yearly, you would divide 72 by 8.

72 ÷ 8 = 9

Therefore, you can project that your savings/investment will double in 9 years.

Weekly Money Management Mini-Project

MATERIALS NEEDED:

Fake Money ($100)	Newspaper (Grocery Section or
Donated Commodities	School Supplies, School Clothes,
	etc.)
Checking Log	Color Pencils and Regular Pencils
Savings Log	Pocket Folder or Binder

Teacher's Instructions:

1. Copy $100 dollar bills and a mixture of other dollar bills or buy fake money. Call the bills Johnson Bucks or use your last name or your school's name.

2. Give each student a $100 bill or give any desired amount of money as a pretend salary that depends on the completion of classwork and homework.

3. Give each student a checkings/outstandings log and a savings log.

4. Supervise this mini-project as a group activity or supervise the mini-project as an individual activity. Instruct the students to record a Starting Balance of $100.

5. Teacher-direct them from their instructions.

6. Organize your materials so that it will be easily accessible each week to the students.

7. Choose one day of the week that is convenient for you to supervise this on-going mini-project.

8. When you feel that they are ready, advance them to our more comprehensive project.

9. Advanced students may start with our financial education workbook: Groom To Be Wealthy: Early Wealthy Management for Kids. This project provides user-friendly step-by-step instructions. You may order it online or by e-mailing. Order on www.MultiplicationShake.com or by e-mailing info@MultiplicationShake.com.

Student's Instructions:

!. Write Starting Balance under the Transaction column. Write $100 under Credit/Deposit. Also, write $100 under Balance. Under the Notes column, write Current Balance.

2. a. Write a check for Charity for 10% of the $100. Deduct that $____ from $100. What is your balance? $____

CHECK WRITING: Write the date. Write Charity or a name of a charity that you would like to support. Write the words for the amount (Ten Dollars and 00 over a bar and 100). Draw a line to Dollars. Write Giving/Sharing on the memo. Sign your name in cursive writing.

2. b. Record the date that the check was written. Write the check number under the check number column. Write Charity or the name of your favorite Charity under the Transaction column. Write 10.00 under the debit column. Subtract. In the Notes column, write Giving/Sharing.

3. Pretend that a transfer to your savings account will take place. Deduct the transfer from the balance.

3. a. The amount of the transfer for the savings deposit will be 10% of $90 which is ____.

3. b. In the checkings/outstandings log, write Emergency Savings in the Transaction column. Write $9.00 under the debit column. Subtract. In the Notes column, write Save for the Unexpected.

4. Record the amount in your savings log. Write the current date. Write Deposit in the Transaction column. Write $9.00 under Credit/Deposit. Also, write $9.00 under Balance. In the Notes column, write Emergency Savings.

5. Use the grocery section of a newspaper to individual students or partners to shop for needs. Use the school clothes and/or the school supplies section, too. Donated food certificates, clothing certificates, etc. may used for purchases.

6. On the back of your savings log, list your needs and costs. Total the amounts correctly. Double check the totals. Maintain or keep at least $10 in your checking account.

7. In your checkings/outstandings log, record the date you purchased your needs.

8. Write DC for this Debit Card transaction in the DC column.

9. Write the name of the store under Transaction. Write the correct total of your needs under the debit column. Subtract.

10. In your checkings/outstandings log, write pretend In Dates in the O/I column. O stands for Outstanding or unpaid transactions. I stands for In Dates or dates transactions are paid by your credit union/bank.

10. a. Place a capital I in the O. Use the green color pencil to mark the I for In Dates and use the green color pencil to write in the following dates in:

Balance – Place capital I in the O in the O/I column. The In Date is the same day it was deposited.

Charity – Place capital I in the O in the O/I column. The In Date is two (2) days after the deposit date.

Emergency Savings – Place capital I in the O in the O/I column. The In Date is two (2) days after the deposit date.

Grocery – Place capital I in the O in the O/I column. The In Date is the same day as the deposit date.

10. b. Write in the In Dates for the savings deposit in your savings log. Use the green color pencil and the same In Date as on the checkings/outstandings log.

11. Next week, write in the current date on this checkings/outstandings log. Write Deposit under Transaction. Write $75 under Credit/Deposit. Add.

12. a. Use your debit card to give to Charity for 10% of $75 which is $____. What is your new balance? $____

12. b. Record the date that the debit card was used. Write DC under the Debit Card column. Write Charity or the name of your favorite Charity under the Transaction column. Write the amount under the debit column. Subtract. In the Notes column, write Giving/Sharing.

13. a. Save 10% of the $75 which is _____. Record the amount In the checkings/outstandings log and record the amount in the savings log. The amount of the savings deposit will be $17.50.

13. b. In the checkings/outstandings log, write Emergency Savings in the Transaction column. Write $7.50 under the debit column. Subtract because this money will be deposited into savings. In the Notes column, write Save for the Unexpected.

14. Record the amount in your savings log. Write the current date. Write Deposit in the Transaction column. Write $7.50 under Credit/Deposit. Add to get your new balance. Write $16.50 under Balance. In the Notes column, write Emergency Savings.

15. Use the grocery section of a newspaper to individual students or partners to shop for needs. Use the school clothes and/or the school supplies section, too. In the back of your savings log, list your needs and costs. Total the amounts correctly. Double check the totals. Maintain or keep more than $10 in your checking account.

16. In your checkings/outstandings log, record the date you purchased your needs.

17. Write DC for this Debit Card transaction in the DC column.

18. Write the name of the store under Transaction. Write the correct total of your needs under the debit column. Subtract.

19. In your checkings/outstandings log, write pretend In Dates in the O/I column. 'O' stands for Outstanding or unpaid transactions. 'I' stands for In Dates or dates transactions are paid by your credit union/bank.

20. a. Place a capital 'I' in the 'O'. Use the green color pencil to mark the 'I' for In Dates and use the green color pencil to write in the following dates in:

Balance – Place capital 'I' in the 'O' in the O/I column. The In Date is the same day it was deposited.

Charity – Place capital 'I' in the 'O' in the O/I column. The In Date is two (2) days after the deposit date.

Emergency Savings – Place capital 'I' in the 'O' in the O/I column. The In Date is two (2) days after the deposit date.

Grocery – Place capital 'I' in the 'O' in the O/I column. The In Date is the same day as the deposit date.

20. b. Write in the In Dates for the savings deposit in your savings log. Use the green color pencil and the same In Date as on the checkings/outstandings log.

21. Next week, write in the current date on this checkings/outstandings log. Write Deposit under Transaction. Write $75 under Credit/Deposit. Add.

22. a. Save 10% of the $175. Record the amount in the checkings/outstandings log and record the amount in the savings log, too. The amount of the savings deposit will be 10% of $175 which is $17.50.

22. b. In the checkings/outstandings log, write Emergency Savings in the Transaction column. Write $17.50 under the debit column. Subtract this money because it will be transferred to the savings account. In the Notes column, write Save for the Unexpected.

23. Record the amount in your savings log. Write the current date. Write Deposit in the Transaction column. Write $17.50 under Credit/Deposit. Add to get your new balance. Write $34 under Balance. In the Notes column, write Emergency Savings.

24. Each week earn and enter a larger deposit and save more. Shop for your needs. Do your recordings immediately. Refer back to numbers 11 – 20.

25. Place your Student's Instructions Sheet, savings log, checkings/outstandings log, green pencil in a pocket folder or a binder. Ask your teacher for another copy of the logs as needed.

26. Manually track and balance your checkbook even if you use a debit card for all of your transactions. The financial skills that you learned in this real life-like project are expected to be transferred to your real life of financial management.

Answer Key - Weekly Money Management Mini-Project

2. $10, $90

3. a. $9, $81

4. $9

5. Self-explanatory (SE)

6. The balance must be at least $10.

7. – 11. Self-explanatory (SE)

12. a. $7.50 Balances will vary.

13. Save $7.50   Balance, $16.50

14. - 21. Self-explanatory (SE)

22. $17.50

23. $34

24. – 26. Self-explanatory (SE)

Name _____ Date _____

Class Store Mini-Project

Focus: Early Money Management   **Profit Margin
          Budgeting
          Check writing
          Balancing
          Tracking Inventory

TEACHER'S DIRECTIONS: Instruct students to read thoroughly. Instruct students to price each item high enough to make a "profit."

I. Read this paragraph until you fully understand the contents.

Class Store Data

Use this information to set up a budget and a table for Lillie Dillie's Class Store. The teacher has $20 in cash. The secretary of the class plans to buy Number 2 pencils for 100 students at 10 cents per unit. The store has room for 50 pens at 10 cents per unit. The store has room for 50 pens at 10 cents per unit. Shelves can hold 5 packets which cost 50 cents per package. Also, eight pocket folders at 20 cents each are needed. Calculate your totals for budgets and tables.

II. Create a Budget for Class Store Supplies

Directions: 1) Get two sheets of paper. 2) Label one sheet "Budget for Lillie Dillie's Class Store" 3) Reread the paragraph and set up your budget for buying pencils, pens, paper, and pocket folders. Your budget must list income ($20) and expenses (things to buy for the store.) Spend under $20.

III. Create a Table for Class Store Supplies

Directions: 1) Use the other sheet of paper and label it "Table for Lillie Dillies's Class Store. 2) Draw a 4 x 6 table. 3) Place the headings for the table are as follows: Items, Cost per Unit, Quantity, and Totals.

Questions:

1. How much did the secretary spend?

2. How much cash is left from the $20?

IV. Write a check to pay the cashier. Balance the checkbook immediately. Record the In Dates in the checkbook register.

IV. Create a Class Store Supplies Inventory Sheet

Draw a 5 X 12 table or use the inventory sheet provided. Monthly, keep track of the inventory of the supplies on a separated inventory sheet.

Directions for each separate Class Store Inventory Sheet are as follows:

I. Set up an inventory sheet for Pencils, dated August 1, 2009. 1) Write August 12, 2009 as a pretend date in the order date column or use the current date. 2) Write 100 in the quantity of supplies ordered column. 3) Write August 24, 2009 in the inventory check date. 4) Write 50 in the supplies on hand column. 5) Write September 2, 2009 in the reorder date column.

II. Set up an inventory sheet for Pens, dated August 1, 2009. 1) Write August 12, 2009 as a pretend date in the order date column or use the current date. 2) Write 50 in the quantity of supplies ordered column. 3) Write August 24, 2009 in the inventory check date. 4) Write 10 in the supplies on hand column. 5) Write September 1, 2009 in the reorder date column.

III. Set up an inventory sheet for Packs of Paper, dated August 1, 2009. 2) Write 5 packs in the quantity of supplies ordered column. 3) Write August 24, 2009 in the inventory check date. 4) Write 1 in the supplies on hand column. 5) Write September 1, 2009 in the reorder date column.

IV. Set up an inventory sheet for Pocket Folders, dated August 1, 2009. 1) Write August 12, 2009 as a pretend date in the order date column or use the current date. 2) Write 100 in the quantity of supplies ordered column. 3) Write August 24, 2009 in the inventory check date. 4) Write 2 in the supplies on hand column. 5) Write September 1, 2009 in the reorder date column.

When it is time to reorder, write another check, balance the checkbook immediately, and record the In Dates as soon as possible. Focus on having supplies on hand or available for the student customers.

Check Writing, Balancing and Tracking In Dates for Class Store

Name _____ Date _____

Complete the checks and record them. Checks/Balance

_____ 33-1   2004
_____ 777
_____   _____

Pay to the
 order of _____ $ _____

_____ Dollars

G Financial Institution
777 Royal Road
Elsewhere, LA 77777

For _____ _____

_____ 33-2   2005
_____ 777
_____   _____

Pay to the
 order of _____ $ _____

_____ Dollars

G Financial Institution
777 Royal Road
Elsewhere, LA 77777

For _____ _____

_____ 33-3   2006
_____ 777
_____   _____

Pay to the
 order of _____ $ _____

_____ Dollars

G Financial Institution
777 Royal Road
Elsewhere, LA 77777

For _____ _____

Transaction Registry for an "X" Cellent Generation

DATE	CASH MO/DC/IDC ACH NUMBER	MO/CASH AMOUNT - TRANSACTION	TWO	DEBIT/ PAYMENT	O/O	DATE	CREDIT/DEPOSIT	BALANCE	NOTES

MultiplicationShake.com
Groom To Be Wealthy

Class Store Supplies Inventory Sheet

Beginning Date: _____   Item: _____

*Copy one inventory sheet per item.

Order Date	Quantity of Supplies Ordered	Inventory Check Date	Supplies On Hand	Reorder Date
1.				
2.				
3.				
4.				
5.				
6.				
7.				
8.				
9.				
10.				
11.				
12.				

Class Store – Answer Key

BUDGET-

Income - $20

Expenses –

Pencils $10.00

Pens $ 5.00

Paper $ 2.50

Pocket Folders $ 1.60

Total $19.10

TABLE – 4 x 6

Items	Cost Per Unit	Quantity	Totals
Pencils	$0.10	100	$10.00
Pens	$0.10	50	$ 5.00
Paper	$0.50 package	5	$ 2.50
Pocket Folders	$0.20	8	$ 1.60
			$19.10

Check Number _____ $20 Starting Balance   Balance $0.90

Inventory – Beginning Supplies – Look back in the Quantity column of the Class Store Table for Supplies to access beginning inventory. Use pretend dates and a pretend number for supplies on hand.

*Copy one inventory sheet per item.

Draw a 5 X 13 table in dimension.

Beginning Date: <u>August 1, 2009</u>   Item: <u>Pencils</u>

Class Store Supplies

Inventory Sheet

Order Date	Quantity of Supplies Ordered	Inventory Check Date	Supplies On Hand	Projected Reorder Date
1. 8/12/09	100	8/24/09	50	9/1/09
2.				
3.				
4.				
5.				
6.				
7.				
8.				
9.				
10.				
11.				
12.				

ATM Machine Role-Play

Lesson to Learn: Track Money, Save Money, Balance Awareness

Characters:

ATM Machine (Sound Effects)　　　Unmarried Couple　　　Doorbell

Setting: Going on a Date

Girlfriend: (on the phone) Girl, he is so cute! He is buffed! I accidentally fell into his chest. (oohh, Girl!)

Boyfriend: (Driving to get this girl every guy in the school wants to date) (on the phone)

Man, this chick has it all. I am going to treat her like the queen she is! Whatever she wants, I am getting it!

OK, man! I'm at her house! I'll hit you up later!

(Presses doorbell) Dingy Dingy Dong Dong

Boyfriend: Hi! You look great! Shall we go?

Girlfriend: Yeah! Good-bye Mom!

Boyfriend : (Opens the door for girlfriend) I got here as soon as I could. We'll have to make a quick stop to the ATM machine! Ah right?

Girlfriend: Whatever!

Boyfriend: ATM Machine makes a broken down noise. (Boyfriend says, "This machine is tripping! (He wipes it off.) This machine is wack! I know my check was deposited two weeks ago!

Come on Baby! Let's kick at Rick's house! He has a theatre in his crib and we can chill and forget about that WACK machine!

Girlfriend: Whatever! I can't tell my friends that we went to big Rick's house. I'll be the laughing stock of the school! Take me home.

More Financial Intelligence, Please – Role Play

Setting: during math class

Alice: I hate all this dumb stuff.

Jo: I don't even know why we need it!

Alice: Why can't we learn more about financial intelligence? Please?

Mrs. Teacher: Well, I'm just using the books they gave me. They don't pay me enough to buying extra stuff for ya'll to complain about.

Word!!

*Discuss what was wrong with each character's response.

Role-Play – Right Way

More Financial Intelligence, Please

Setting: (during math class)

Alice: Yeah, check this out! This is what I'm talking about!

Jo: (eyes light up) My parents were just saying we need a subject that teaches financial literacy everyday! For real though...

Mrs. Teacher: Well, I believe in teaching the state standards. You haven't gotten a good education, if you haven't been taught to "budget". I swear if you don't budget, you'll be living just above broke.

Alice and Jo: (say together) Thank you, Mrs. Teacher! We are going to have more financial intelligence!

You Have A Choice – Role Play

Setting (pacing the floor worrying, groaning, regretting financial decisions.)

Bo: Ah!! Ah!! Ah!! I wished I had listened. I thought it wouldn't be this bad!

Ah!!! Ah!!! Ah!!!

Setting (gaiting happily excited about financial decisions) (bright eyed)

Jo: Aha!! Aha!!! Aha!!!

I'm really, really glad I made this decision. I made some gains!! This is really, really working!

My money is really, really working for me!!

Aaa!!! Aaa!!! Aaa!!!

Questions for Discussion:

1. Which person is healthier? Explain.

2. Which person is wealthier? Explain.

3. Explain the possible differences in the choices that each person made.

4. How has this role-play influenced your choice for handling money?

5. Who is a good person to talk to before one begins to gamble or become a shopaholic?

Budget Disagreement – Role Play

College Sweethearts

Guy: Let's get married! Nothing will ever separate us!

Lady: You know I've been waiting for this moment!

Guy: We'll have a quiet justice of the peace wedding! After all, we are in college, Baby!

Lady: Oh No Honey! (Neck working) No! I just can't do it small! I don't live by a budget! Do you know who my daddy is?

Guy: (hold forehead and look down and deeply disturbed) I am glad I found out this out before I married you! I can't marry a woman with who has no budgeting sense! What do you think? Do you think money grows on trees?

Discussion:

1) What has happened to those college sweethearts?
2) How can they come to a workable compromise?

Engage in conversations about "budgeting".

Creative Writing Extension Activity: Assign partners and instruct to create the correct way to handle the plans for the wedding.

Financial Infidelity – Role Play

Setting: (Standing in the forum near the front door. Joe is about to go gamble.)

Characters: married couple, Joe and Bo

Bo: (wife) Joe, you came up in here at 4 o'clock this morning! Where are you going now?

Joe: (husband) Woman, it ain't your business when and where I go! You better get on away from here.

Bo: Don't put your hands on me and you better not lose our house note money!

Joe: Excuse me! You think I don't know it! You, see you! You hid a $300 dress under the bed; hid a $200 pair of silver high heels; and hid a $20 pair of panty hose with snakes running up and down your legs high up in the corner of the closet.

Look like to me, you better cash in dress and stuff! You try to put me on a guilt trip!

Discussion Questions

1. What is infidelity?

2. Do you think that it is common? Does it break up marriages?

3. What the problems in this marriage?

Creative Writing: Write the correct way to handle the problems in this marriage.

Act it out correctly. Discuss the correct approaches.

Two Day Expense Sheets

Name _____

Choose two days in which you will spend money wisely. Save money consistently per pay check.

Dates covered _____

Needs

Item	Cost
1. _____	_____
2. _____	_____
3. _____	_____
4. _____	_____
Total	_____

Fixed Expenses – Day 1

Item	Cost
1. _____	_____
2. _____	_____
3. _____	_____
4. _____	_____
Total	_____

Fixed Expenses – Day 2

Item   Cost

1. _____   _____

2. _____   _____

3. _____   _____

4. _____   _____

                                   Total   _____

Financial Goals

1.

2.

3.

Sample Budgets

Kids/Teens/Tys Budget

Directions: Draw or cut out pictures from the sheets, magazines, or www.google.com images. Set up this hands-on budget on a large paper.

ALLOWANCE	SAMPLE	PERSONAL	DATE
Pictures of Chore(s)	Amount	Amount	(1st, etc.)
Total Allowance	$20.00	_____	____

Draw the chore you performed with integrity in order to earn your allowance. Draw the needs you will purchase with the $20. Stay within your budget.

NEEDS OR EXPENSES

Pictures	Give/Save/Spend	Amount	Amount

Positive Scarcity Budget

Partial Monthly BUDGET PRIORITY

INCOME	
SALARY	
RENT COLLECTION	$1000
TRUST FUND	$ 500
TOTAL INCOME	$3150

EXPENSES	
TITHES AND CHARITY	$ 315
SHORT TERM EMERGENCY	$ 100
INVEST SYSTEMATICALLY MONTHLY	$ 100
HOME MORTGAGE	$ 800

Positive Abundance Budget

There is an over-abundance of capital for everything.

INCOME

Monthly Salary	$1500	(Connection to Passion)
Passive Income	$2100	(Build and Sell Businesses, Rental Property)
Dividends	+ 500	(Cash Investments)
Total Income	$4100	

EXPENSES

Faith, Hope and Love	$410
Children's Wish List	$$
Walmart Stock Certificates	$$
Merrill Lynch (Cash Management Account)	$$
Goldman Sach	$$
Scholarship Foundation	$$
Taxes	$$
Home	$$
Cars	$$
Rental Property Repairs	$$
Renters Pay Your Mortgage	$$
Cell Phones (Business)	$$
Black American Express Card	$$
Consultation Fees (Money Growth)	$$
Utility Expenses Association Fees	$$
Total Expenses	$$

Negative Scarcity Budget (Partial Monthly Budget)

INCOME	
SALARY	$1,650
RENT COLLECTION	$0
TRUST FUND	$0
TOTAL INCOME	$1,650
EXPENSES	
TITHES/CHARITY	$0
EMERGENCY SAVINGS	$ 0
INVEST MONTHLY	
SYSTEMATICALLY	$0
HOME	$0
RENTAL HOME	
PAYMENT	$1,000
USED CADDY	$ 400
EDUCATION LOAN	$ 20
GROUP INSURANCE COVERAGE	
(LIFE, MEDICAL, DENTAL)	$0
PAY DAY LOAN	$ 200
PERSONAL LOAN	$ 50
FASHION GIRL CARD	$ 10
PARTIAL MO. EXPENSES	$1,680

INCLUDE UTILITIES, GAS, FOOD, AND OTHER EXPENSES

Check Writing, Balancing and Tracking

Name _____   Date _____

                                                                    Checks/Balance

Complete the checks and record them.

_____   33-1   2004
_____   777
_____   _____

Pay to the
  order of _____ $ _____

_____ Dollars

G Financial Institution
777 Royal Road
Elsewhere, LA 77777

For _____   _____

_____   33-2   2005
_____   777
_____   _____

Pay to the
  order of _____ $ _____

_____ Dollars

G Financial Institution
777 Royal Road
Elsewhere, LA 77777

For _____   _____

_____   33-3   2006
_____   777
_____   _____

Pay to the
  order of _____ $ _____

_____ Dollars

G Financial Institution
777 Royal Road
Elsewhere, LA 77777

For _____   _____

Transaction Registry for an "X" Cellent Generation

DATE	CASH MO/DC/CC ACH NUMBER	MO/CASH AMOUNT - TRANSACTION	TWO	DEBIT/ PAYMENT	C/O	DATE	CREDIT/DEPOSIT	BALANCE	NOTES

MultiplicationShake.com
Groom To Be Wealthy

Math

Measurements – Fruity Smoothies & Tea Cakes

(classroom fun)

<u>Fruity Smoothies</u>

1 ½ cup Ice   5 Strawberries

1 Banana (sliced)   ½ cup Apple or Favorite Juice

Ice Cream (optional)

Blend on high all ingredients. Stop the blender and stir. Blend until all ice is crushed. Relax and enjoy your smoothie.

Makes 12 ounces.

<u>Tea Cakes</u>

2 cups of flour   2 teaspoons cinnamon

1 cup of sugar   1 – 2 cups milk

Dash of salt   2 teaspoons lemon juice

In a large bowl, mix all dry ingredients. Add the lemon juice. Add small amounts of milk at a time. Tea cakes need to be kneaded and rolled out. Cut the dough the size of biscuits and bake them on 400 degrees until golden brown.

Money and Percentages Chart and Games

Pictures	Money	Fractions of A $1.00/Dollar	Decimals	Percents	Fractions	Reduce to Lowest Terms
	$0.05	1/20	0.05	5%	5/100	1/20
	$0.10	1/10	0.1	10%	10/100	1/10
	$0.20	1/5	0.20	20%	20/100	1/5
	$0.30	3/10	0.30	30%	30/100	3/10
	$0.80	4/5	0.80	80%	80/100	4/5
	$0.25	1/4	0.25	25%	25/100	1/4
	$0.50	1/2	0.50	50%	50/100	1/2
	$0.75	3/4	0.75	75%	75/100	3/4
	$1.00	4/4	1	100%	100/100	1

Credits to Leanoria R. Johnson and MultiplicationShake.com

*Under the column labeled Pictures, instruct students to draw in the coins or cut and paste in coins. A dollar bill is acceptable, too.

Musical Chairs

Focus Skill: Converting Decimals to Percents

Materials Needed: Instrumental Music on "The Multiplication Shake" CD, CD player, six chairs, seven students, decimals written on large sticky post-its, marker, white board or poster board etc.

Directions: Write six decimals from the chart on six different large sticky post-it notes. Place the six chairs in a circle. Stick one sticky note under each chair. Play the music and stop the music. The student who does not have a chair must choose one chair, pull it aside, remove the sticky note, read the decimal, and convert it to a percent. Post up the decimal and write the percent by or under the decimal. Explain the procedure, too.

Variation of Musical Chairs

Focus Skill: Building a Personal Budget

Materials Needed: A partially built budget displayed on an easel, parts of the budget are typed or written on sentence strips or large sticky post-its, marker, white board or poster board, decimals written on large sticky post-its, marker, white board or poster board, instrumental music on "The Multiplication Shake" CD, CD player, six chairs, seven students, etc.

Directions: Write missing parts of a budget on sentence strips or large sticky notes. Place the six chairs in a circle. Stick one of the sentence strips under each chair. Play the music and stop the music. The student who does not have a chair must "build the budget." He or she will read what is on the sentence strip that is under the chair. Display the part of the budget on the poster or the white board that displays the partial budget. Explain the priority of the placement, too.

Deep Fish

Focus Skill: Fraction Equivalents

Materials Needed: Homemade or a magnetic toy fishing pole, paper clips, magnetic toy fish or home-made fish, adhesive circles, markers, and a money and percentage chart.

Directions: Write six different fractions from the chart on six different small sticky circles. Place the six chairs in a circle. Stick one sticky note on each side of each fish. Play the music and stop the music. The student who does not have a chair must Deep Fish. He or she will fish for one fish, pull it up, read the fraction, write it on the whiteboard and reduce the fraction to the lowest terms. Explain the procedure, too.

Jump Rope

Focus Skill: Fraction Equivalents

Use the money and chart to convert the fraction of a $1.00 to a fraction that has 100 as the denominator.

 Materials Needed: Instrumental Music for "I Love D-I-V-I-S-I-O-N" which is on "The Multiplication Shake" CD, jump rope, fractions written on large sticky post-its, marker, and tape.

Directions: Write six fractions of a dollar from the chart on six different large sticky post-it notes. Tape the post-it notes down. As a student jumps rope, he or she must read the fraction and give the equivalent. Play the music and stop the music when the student stops jumping. Post up the fraction of a dollar and the answer that has 100 in the denominator on a whiteboard. Read both fractions. Explain the procedure, too.

Variation for Jump Rope

Focus Skill: Convert Percents to Decimals

Directions: Use the money and percentage chart. Write percents on post-it notes. Challenge students to convert the percents to decimals.

Hot Dog

Focus Skill: Counting Money

Materials Needed: Instrumental Music for "I Love D-I-V-I-S-I-O-N" which is on "The Multiplication Shake" CD, a stuffed dog, CD player.

Directions: Use the Pictures column to teach "counting money". Play the music and pass the Hot Dog. Whoever has the stuffed dog when the music stops, must say three different combinations to make 50 cents. Play the music, pass the Hot Dog, and stop the music. Whoever has the dog, make three combinations of 25 cents. Continue the game with $1.00, 75 cents. etc.

Variation of Hot Dog: Teach Number Words

Additional Materials Needed: One adhesive circle

Directions: Look at the numbers on the money chart and say and write the number words that someone places an adhesive circle by. Play the music, pass the Hot Dog, and say a number and write number words. Keep the game going.

Variation of Hot Dog: Teach Setting Financial Goals

Additional Materials Need: Copy or a Power Point of Financial Goals

Directions: Flash a visual (3 seconds) of 5 to 8 financial goals such as "I will budget my money each pay period." Instruct students to look at all the goals. Cover all of the goals. Then play the music, pass the Hot Dog, and stop the music. Whoever has the Hot Dog, must recite a financial goal. No financial goal may be repeated.

Name _____   Date _____

Lillie Dillie Picture Math - Addition

Skill: Addition

Directions: Draw pictures and add. Draw the answer. Use complete sentences to answer the question.

1. Draw 3 tea cakes and 3 chocolate cookies.

_____ + _____ = _____

How many cookies do you have in all?

_____

2. Draw 2 nickels and 4 quarters.

_____ + _____ = _____

How many coins do you have in all?

_____

3. Count the value of the two nickels and four quarters.

_____

4. Draw 5 smoothies. Price them at $2.50 each.

_____

How much do they cost all together?

_____

Name _____   Date _____

Lillie Dillie Picture Math - Subtraction

Skill: Subtraction

Directions: Draw pictures and subtract. Draw an "X" to mark out pictures. "X" out pictures from left to right.

1. Draw 9 tea cakes. "X" out 7.

_____ = _____

How many tea cakes are left?

_____

2. Draw 10 quarters. "X" out 3.

_____ = _____

How many coins do you have left?

_____

3. Count the value of the quarters that are left. How much is it?

_____

4. Draw 10 smoothies. Price them at $2.50 each. Subtract ½ of the total.

_____

How much do they cost all together? What is half of the total?

_____

Five (5) Basic Steps to Solve Word Problems

1. Read carefully and figure out what you have been asked to do. Rephrase the question in a way that you understand.

2. Draw pictures, sets of lines, or groups of circles to help you use visuals to solve the problem.

3. Think about what you already know about the concept that is related to the problem. Identify unnecessary information and numbers that don't help you answer the question that is asked of you. Look for clue words like:

Find the sum. (Which means add)

How many altogether? (Which means add)

Find the difference. (Which means subtract)

How many less? (Which means subtract)

Two times as many. (Which means multiply)

What percent of? (Which means multiply)

How many will each get? (Which means divide)

What are the equal parts? (Which means divide)

"x " is what you will solve for in equations.

Find the probability means find the likely chance of something happening.

4. Explore and set up the solution that best solves this problem. You may need a number sentence, an equation, etc.

5. Go back over the question and go back to each step you wrote to solve the problem. Make sure you answer all parts of the question. Check your answer.

Name _____   Date _____

Word Problems

Directions. Read each problem. Write whether you will add, subtract, multiply, or divide. Then actually show your work.

1. The track runners won 9 blue ribbons and 3 red ribbons. How many ribbons did they win in all?

_____

2. Four cats and 6 dogs were chosen as "Best Pet." How many pets were in the final event?

_____

3. The highest hill is 120 inches high. The smallest hill is 100 inches high. What is the difference in height between the two hills?

_____

4. Mike chose 5 bunches of grapes. There were 4 grapes in each bunch. How many grapes did Mike have altogether?

_____

5. Mrs. Joe filled each of the 5 bags with 2 lemons. How many lemons did she buy?

_____

6. There are 30 marbles. Six children must share them. How many marbles will each child get?

_____

"The Multiplication Shake- Multiplication Tables"

I know my multiplication tables. You can do the easy ones just like me.

0 x 1 = 0

0 times any number is 0.

_____

1 x 1 = 1

1 times any number is that number.

_____

2 x 1 = 2	2 + 2 = 4	4 x 1 = 4
2 x 2 = 4	4 + 4 = 8	4 x 2 = 8
2 x 3 = 6	6 + 6 = 12	4 x 3 = 12

Add 2 to the previous answer.

Double the products to get the 4's.

_____

3 x 1 = 3	3 + 3= 6	6 x 1 = 6
3 x 2 = 6	6 + 6 = 12	6 x 2 = 12
3 x 3 = 9		
3 x 4 = 12		
3 x 5 = 15		

Double any product of the 3's and get the products of the 6's. Keep it going. Learn to double and save yourself some trouble.

4 x 1 = 4	4 +4 = 8	8 x 1 = 8
4 x 2 = 8	8 + 8 = 16	8 x 2 = 16

4 x 3 = 12

4 x 4 = 16

4 x 5 = 20

Double any product of the 4's and get the products of the 8's. Keep it going.

Learn to double and save yourself some trouble.

___

Use what you know to do a little more!

5 x 1 = 5	Add 1 Get 6	6 x 1 = 6	Add 1 Get 7	7 x 1 = 7
5 x 2 = 10	Add 2 Get 12	6 x 2 = 12	Add 2 Get 14	7 x 2 = 14
5 x 3 = 15	Add 3 Get 18	6 x 3 = 18	Add 3 Get 21	7 x 3 = 21
5 x 4 = 20	Add 4 Get 24	6 x 4 = 24	Add 4 Get 28	7 x 4 = 28
5 x 5 = 25	Add 5 Get 30	6 x 5 = 30	Add 5 Get 35	7 x 5 = 35

Look at the pattern 1, 2, 3, and on and on.

Use what you know to do a little more! Keep it going! Try your hand at adding the multiplicand! (5)   (6)   (7)

___

8 x 1 = 8	Add 1 Get 9	9 x 1 = 9
8 x 2 = 16	Add 2 Get 18	9 x 2 = 18
8 x 3 = 24	Add 3 Get 27	9 x 3 = 27
8 x 4 = 32	Add 4 Get 36	9 x 4 = 36
8 x 5 = 40	Add 5 Get 45	9 x 5 = 45

Use what you know to do a little more! Keep it going! Try your hand at adding the multiplicand! (8)   (9)

___

The 10's are super easy, too.

10 x 1 = 10

10 x 2 = 20

10 x 3 = 30

10 x 4 = 40

10 x 5 = 50

Use what you know to do a little more! Keep it going! Try your hand at adding the multiplicand! (10)

---

11 x 1 = 11	Add 1 Get 12	12 x 1 = 12
11 x 2 = 22	Add 2 Get 24	12 x 2 = 24
11 x 3 = 33	Add 3 Get 36	12 x 3 = 36
11 x 4 = 44	Add 4 Get 48	12 x 4 = 48
11 x 5 = 55	Add 5 Get 60	12 x 5 = 60

Use what you know to do a little more! Keep it going! Try your hand at adding the multiplicand! (11)   (12)

---

13 x 1= 13	Add 1 Get 14	14 x 1 = 14
13 x 2 = 26	Add 2 Get 28	14 x 2 = 28
13 x 3 = 39	Add 3 Get 42	14 x 3 = 42
13 x 4 = 52	Add 4 Get 56	14 x 4 = 56
13 x 5 = 65	Add 5 Get 70	14 x 5 = 70
13 x 6 = 78	Add 6 Get 84	14 x 6 = 84
13 x 7 = 91	Add 7 Get 98	14 x 7 = 98

13 x 8 = 104   14 x 8 = 112

13 x 9 = 117   14 x 9 = 126

13 x 10 = 130   14 x10 = 140

13 x 11 = 143   14 x 11 = 154

13 x 12 = 156   14 x 12 = 168

13 x 13 = 169   14 x 13 = 182

13 x 14 = 182   14 x 14 = 196

You are so smart! Now, make some flash cards!

Multiplication Step-by-Step Instructions

Two-Digit by Two-digit
Multiplication

```
  34   Multiplicand
X 12   Multiplier
  68
+340
 408   Product
```

STEPS

First, start by multiplying the 2 by the 4. Two is the multiplier. Four is the multiplicand. Both numbers are in ones place.

$2 \times 4 = 8$

Write the 8 under ones place.

- Go back to the multiplier 2. Slide up and over to the left to 30. Multiply 2 times 30.

    $2 \times 30 = 60$

    Write only 6 under tens place.

- Now, start multiplying by the 10. Ten is a multiplier. Ten is in tens place. Multiply 10 times 4 = 40. Write the 0 under ones place. Write 4 under tens place.

- Multiply 10 times 30 = 300. Write the 3 under hundred's place.

- Write the + (plus) sign, draw a line, and add starting at ones place.

Hundreds	Tens	Ones	
	60	8	300
+300	+40	+0	100
300	100	8	+ 8
			408

Name _____ Date _____

Multiplication Practice Sheet – page 1

Sample in the Math Music CD – "The Multiplication Shake" on "The Multiplication Shake" CD

COLOR CODE: 2-RED   1-BLUE   4-GREEN   3-ORANGE
12-MULTIPLIER   34-MULTIPLICAND   408-PRODUCT

```
      34
    x 12
     168
   + 340
     408
```

TO CHECK:

```
        34
   12 | 408
      - 36↓
        48
       -48
         0
```

*The product 408 divided by the multiplier 12 is 34. The quotient 34 is the same as the multiplicand 34. Therefore, the product 408 is correct.

DIRECTIONS: Color code the problems. Work out the problem. Check your answer. Use another sheet of paper.

1. 43	2. 32	3. 33	4. 44	5. 22	6. 12
x 22	x 31	x 21	x 10	x 20	x 12

7. 67	8. 58	9. 41	10. 44	11. 46	12. 20
x 10	x 11	x 22	x 12	x 11	x 10

Name _____ Date _____

Multiplication Practice Sheet – page 2

Sample in the Math Music CD – "The Multiplication Shake" on "The Multiplication Shake" CD

COLOR CODE: 2-RED 1-BLUE 4-GREEN 3-ORANGE
12-MULTIPLIER 34-MULTIPLICAND 408-PRODUCT

```
     34
   x 12
    168
  + 340
    408
```

TO CHECK:

```
        34
     ┌──────
  12 │ 408
     │
     - 36↓
     ──────
        48

       -48
     ──────
         0
```

*The product 408 divided by the multiplier 12 is 34. The quotient 34 is the same as the multiplicand 34. Therefore, the product 408 is correct.

DIRECTIONS: Color code the problems. Work out the problem. Check your answer. Use another sheet of paper.

1. 13	2. 31	3. 21	4. 46	5. 22	6. 11
X 2 3	x 31	x 21	x 10	x 22	x 11

7. 78	8. 68	9. 42	10. 43	11. 46	12. 20
x 10	x 11	x 32	x 12	x 11	x 10

Division Step-by-Step Instructions

DIVISION WITH NO REMAINDER

```
          34                                  To Check:
   12  | 408                                      34
       |                                        X 12
                                                ────
       - 36↓                                      6 8
                                                +3 4 0
         48                                     ──────
       - 48                                     4 0 8
       ────
          0
```

(12 → DIVISOR   408 → DIVIDEND   34 → QUOTIENT)

Do   1. **DIVIDE** evenly 12 into 40. Get as close to 40 as possible.

               2. Write the answer 3 above the 0 in 408.

Monkeys   3. **MULTIPLY** 3 times 12. Write the 36 under the 40.

Ski?   4. **SUBTRACT** 36 from 40 and get 4.

               5. Write the 4 under the 6 in 36.

               6. Draw an arrow and bring down the 8. The 48 is the new dividend.

Do   7. **DIVIDE** 12 into 48 and get 4.

               8. Write the 4 above the 8 in 408.

Mo nkeys   9. **MULTIPLY** 4 times 12 and get 48.

Ski   10. **SUBTRACT** 48 from 48 and get 0.

               11. Write the 0 under the 8 and not in the quotient.

               12. The final quotient is 34.

Ci Ci?   13. CHECK your answer.

Name _____ Date _____

Division Practice Sheet – page 1

Sample in the Math Music CD –"I Love D-I-V-I-S-I-O-N" on "The Multiplication Shake" CD

COLOR CODE: 12-GREEN   408-ORANGE   34-RED

12-DIVISOR   408-DIVIDEND   34-QUOTIENT

```
        34
   12 ⟌ 408
      - 36↓
        48
       -48
         0
```

The product 408 is the same as the dividend 408. Therefore, your quotient 34 is correct.

DIRECTIONS: Color code the problems. Work out the problem. Check your answer.

1.

14 ⟌ 308

2.

16 ⟌ 352

3.

15 ⟌ 330

4.

20 ⟌ 640

Name _____ Date _____

Division Practice Sheet – page 2

Sample in the Math Music CD –"I Love D-I-V-I-S-I-O-N" on "The Multiplication Shake" CD

COLOR CODE: 12-GREEN   408-ORANGE   34-RED

12-DIVISOR 408-DIVIDEND 34-QUOTIENT

```
          34
      ┌────────
  12  │ 408
      │ - 36↓
      │  ────
          48
         -48
         ────
           0
```

The product 408 is the same as the dividend 408. Therefore, your quotient 34 is correct.

DIRECTIONS: Color code the problems. Work out the problem. Check your answer.

1.

```
  44 │ 528
```

2.

```
  15 │ 345
```

3.

```
  18 │ 396
```

4.

```
  30 │ 930
```

Answer Key

"The Multiplication Shake" Math Music CD

Multiplication and Division Problems are **WITHIN THE SONGS**

Problems in "The Multiplication Shake" Song

1. 408   2. 506 3. 363   4. 550   5. 429

Problems in "I LOVE D-I-V-I-S-I -O-N".

1. 34   2. 19   3. 20   4. 71   5. 61

Multiplication and Division **Practice Sheets**

Multiplication Practice Sheets

Page 1

1. 946	2. 992	3. 693	4. 440	5. 440	6. 144
7. 670	8. 638	9. 902	10. 408	11. 506	12. 400

Page 2

1. 286	2. 961	3. 441	4. 460	5. 484	6. 121
7. 780	8. 748	9. 1,344	10. 516	11. 506	12. 200

Division Practice Sheets

Page 1

1. 22	2. 22	3. 22	4. 32

Page 2

1. 12	2. 23	3. 22	4. 31

Reading and Writing

Name _____ Date _____

Lillie Dillie's Childhood

Skill: Summarize

Directions: Read the chapter thoroughly.

1. Summarize the chapter in your own words.

_____

_____

_____

_____

_____

_____

_____

_____

_____

2. What does this chapter remind you of?

_____

_____

_____

_____

_____

_____

3. What could be another ending for the chapter?

_____

_____

_____

_____

_____

_____

_____

_____

Name _____   Date _____

Lillie Dillie Rhymes

Skill: Rhyming Words

Rhyming words sound alike. They may have a different beginning letter and the same ending sound.

Directions: Skim chapter 1 of <u>Lillie Dillie Start Wealthy</u> for words that rhyme with the words listed in numbers 1 – 10. Write the paragraph and the page number of where the words were found.

1. mouth - _____ page _____ paragraph _____

2. matches - _____ page _____ paragraph _____

3. Indiana - _____ page _____ paragraph _____

4. ironic - _____ page _____ paragraph _____

5. advances - _____ page _____ paragraph _____

6. Earl - _____ page _____ paragraph _____

7. malicious - _____ page _____ paragraph _____

8. tomatoes - _____ page _____ paragraph _____

9. mange - _____ page _____ paragraph _____

10. alive - _____ page _____ paragraph _____

Write complete sentences using the rhyming word pairs.

1.

2.

3.

4.

5.

6.

7.

8.

9.

10.

Define each word below. After you write the meaning of the word, write how you are able to relate to each word.

1. economic –

2. mange –

3. ironic –

4. malicious –

5. change -

Answer Key for Lillie Dillie Rhymes

1. mouth   South   page 6 paragraph 1

2. matches patches   page 6 paragraph 1

3. Indiana   banana   page 6 paragraph 2 and

                                page 11 paragraph 2

4. ironic   stomach   page 8 top of the page

5. advances circumstances page 6 paragraph 2

6. Earl   girl   page 6 paragraph 1

7. malicious delicious   page 7 paragraph 1

8. tomatoes potatoes   page 6 paragraph 2

9. mange   change   page 7 paragraph 2 and

                                in the question on page 7

10. alive   arrived   page 8 paragraph 1

1. economic – way of life; power of money; based on making, selling, and using goods and services

2. mange – a contagious skin disease usually of domestic animals in which there is itching and loss of hair

3. ironic – means the opposite of what one really intends to happen

4. malicious – doing mean things for pleasure

5. change – money returned after a payment is made; money in coins; become different

Name _____ Date _____

Smoothie Time

Directions: Reread the section about Lillie Dillie and Mrs. Boykin preparing fruity smoothies. Imagine each step of the scene in your mind. Draw the scene.

Retell that part of the story using descriptive words.

_____

_____

_____

_____

_____

_____

Application:

Ask your father to create fun memories with you and your family every Friday after school. Take pictures of this fun experience. Use the recipes on page 89 of <u>Lillie Dillie Start Wealthy</u>. Write about your family experience.

_____

_____

_____

_____

Name _____   Date _____

Playwriting

Directions: Beginning writers may form a group and write a play depicting two scenes after reading chapters.

Directions: Advanced writers may convert the literacy part into a live play with music, props, etc. Outline your play.

Make a video of the play. Invite the entire school to see the play.

Invite the author to enjoy your creativity.

Email Leanoria@MultiplicationShake.com.

Name _____ Date _____

Outlining

Directions: Reread the story. Fill in the outline using the main topics as your guide.

I.   Lillie Dillie had three key ladies in her childhood.

      A.

      B.

      C.

II.   Lillie Dillie could have possibly been stressed out about

      A.

      B.

      C.

III.   Pudgy had

      A.

      B.

IV.   Mr. Buckeye

      A.

      B.

Name _____ Date _____

Critical Thinking

Directions: Use the information in Lillie Dillie in order to answer this question.

1. Mrs. Boykin was not a small lady. Why do you think she gave Lillie Dillie small portions of cookies for her snack? Illustrate Mrs. Boykin serving Lillie Dillie small portions under your explanation.

   _____

   _____

   _____

2. Mr. Buckeye was dedicated to helping young people learn how to save money. What experiences might have influenced Mr. Buckeye's dedication to his passion to help young people? Under your explanation, illustrate Mr. Buckeye speaking to a large group of young people. Write scripts for Mr. Buckeye.

   _____

   _____

   _____

Name _____ Date _____

Healthy Eating

Directions: Illustrate Lillie Dillie eating a light snack.

Retell that part of the story.

_____

_____

_____

Application: Think about your after school snack. What is your healthy snack? Is your snack full of sugar, salt, grains, or fruits? Explain.

_____

_____

_____

Name _____ Date _____

Service Learning

Directions: Illustrate or draw pictures of two different illustrations. Show Lillie Dillie running errands for Mrs. Boykin and Mrs. Wilson. Describe your illustration.

Service Learning: Who can you do a small task for in your school, neighborhood, or church?

_____

_____

"Do the Do"

Skills: Hyperbole, Idiom, Repetition, Multiple Meanings, The Arts (drama, dance, draw)

Do develop All-Star character and dress the part.
Do your passion with an ocean-wide heart.
Do take care of your body parts.
Do value good health.
Do count it as your wealth.
Do respect yourself first.
Do give respect away and not your purse.

Do the do!   (Do a wiggly dance!)

Do give thanks and live according to the good book.
Do divide your time, money, commodities, expertise, and hook with others.
Do enjoy life. Read, travel, and soak up the sun.
Do use music to enhance educational fun.
Do drain the cup of sorrow.
Do seek a better tomorrow.
Do believe that the best is yet to come and there is no need to borrow.

Do the do!   (Do a wiggly dance!)

Do multiply your money so it will grow.
Do this and you will attract more.
Do what is ethical and moral.
Do what causes no one else sorrow.
Do what you do well.
Do expect to hear that's swell.
Do the do that is true to the true you.

Do the do!   (Do a wiggly dance!)

Leanoria Johnson

"Do the Do" Activities for Eight (8) Days

Skills: Hyperbole, Idiom, Repetition, Multiple Meanings, The Arts (drama, dance, draw)

1. A. Play instrumental music as all of the students read.

B. Design and color a Book of Poetry cover. Write on lined paper 5 to 6 lines each day until the poem is copied. Some may copy the entire poem in one day.

2. A. Assign dancers to dance the rhythm and assign other students to choral read. Form a poetry circle. Start the music, Choral readers and dancers partner. Teacher reads in the center of the circle. After the count of 3, let the fun begin.

B. Box the stanzas and number the lines. ABC order and define: enhance, morals, commodities, true, expertise,

3. A. Repeat the poetry circle fun.

B. Choose lines for role playing, charades, drawings, etc. Draw role plays and describe what is happening.

4. A. Switch roles of dancers and readers, if students want to.

B. Make a connection to the poem. Explain in 5 or more sentences.

C. Write rhyming word pairs.

5. A. Dance and choral read.

B. Locate the words that have multiple meanings. (divide, hook, true, swell) Write the meanings of each word and sentences to match the meanings.

6. A. Choral read the poem with instrumental music.

B. Locate the hyperbole (exaggeration) and the idiom (peculiar expression). How does the hyperbole relate to you or not relate to you? Explain what the idiomatic expression in the poem means.

Ocean-wide heart is the hyperbole. Dress the part is the idiomatic expression.

7. A. Choral read the poem with instrumental music.

B. What pattern do you see in the poem? Write a similar heart-felt poem with a unique pattern. Sign the poem. Enlarge and post for others to enjoy. Read over school's intercom system.

Come Alive Activities

Come Alive activities provide meaningful applications of ideas in the book. Stimulate readers of this book to enjoy making characters and activities come alive! Guide the readers in purposefully planning these activities so that they may have similar experiences as the characters in the book. The suggested activities are as follows:

1) Engage in family devotions with the purpose of building spiritual wealth.

2) Establish a Parents/Kids Club and visit your local credit union or bank to set up systematic deposits in a savings account and/or an investments account. Begin the process of building financial wealth.

3) Set up groups and give students directions for completing visual boards and budgets N' crafts activities. Collect pictures from google.com (images), magazines, or photos.

4) Make a poster and announce a "Multiplication Shake" Dance Contest! Video the contestants dance the most creative to the "Multiplication Shake CD"! Award the winner an opportunity to dance on the stage of a renowned public television station!

5) Host a Celebrate Math Day! Set up different games in different classrooms or a gymnasium. Ring a bell and direct students to rotate to a new math game each time the bell rings. Award the students who earn the highest scores.

6) Announce a cheerleader competition for the best cheer to the tune of "I Love D-I-V-I-S-I-O-N".

7) Cultivate your child's passion, people skills, and talents. Turn what your child loves into a prosperous business.

8) Use the recipes in the Teaching Aides section of the book to prepare smoothies and teacakes. Make up word problems from the recipes.

9) Take a trip to Shreveport, Louisiana to see the shotgun house where Lillie Dillie grew up. Collect some dirt to make mud cakes and samples of wild plants that were greens that Lillie Dillie pretended to cook.

Arts and Crafts

Visual Boards

Directions:

Write your goals in the frame. Your goals will need to be specific, observable, and attainable. Include a time for your goals to be accomplished. Begin your goals with: I will …

Update your goals as you finish them and set more goals.

 Draw or cut and paste in pictures of what will fulfill your "dreams."

Cut pictures out of magazines, newspapers and google.com some of your images.

You may choose to buy a scrapbook for your goals and pictures. In that case, write your goals above your pictures.

Date _____

Budgets N' Crafts

Parent or Teacher Directions

Student should follow the directions below.

Use 11 x 17 construction paper. Use pretend or real numbers.

Make two columns. Title the left hand column ALLOWANCE. Title the right hand column AMOUNT.

	ALLOWANCE	AMOUNT
Picture	Chore/_____	$ _____
	(Name of Chore)	
		Total Allowance $ _____

*Place a picture of you performing a chore with integrity. Write the name of the chore such as dishwashing, mowing the lawn, putting away toys. etc. Write the dollar amount.

Draw a line across the paper to separate the top section (ALLOWANCES) from the bottom section (NEEDS).

Make two columns. Title the left hand column NEEDS. Title the right hand column AMOUNT. Draw or cut and paste in pictures of your needs. Stay within your budget. Place more needs under number 1, like savings, investments, computers, etc.

	NEEDS	AMOUNT
1. Picture	Church/Tithes/Charity/_____	$
2. Picture	Credit Union/Bank	$

Name _____   Date _____

Money Wall Plaques

Focus: Set goals to save money.

Materials Needed:

Paper Plates	Scissors
Bills or Coins (Play or Real)	Glue
Crayons or Markers	String or Plaque Holder (stand)

Directions: Write one or several financial goals. Make a decorative border with bills or coins. Draw a picture or cut and paste a picture of what you are saving for. Decorate your plaque and hang it on the wall or place it on a stand.

Smiley Face Cookies

Focus: Improve understanding of math concepts

Materials Needed: dough, icing, paper, pencil, and ruler

Purchase plain cookie dough. Follow directions that are on the package. Place a face on the cookies with raisins.

Math variation: Make math sentences with the cookies. You may add, subtract, multiply, or divide with the cookies.

Art Variation: Buy colored icing and make math designs on the cookies. Answer questions about the designs such as the following:

1) How many sides are in the design?

2) Are the designs congruent?

3) What is the circumference of different cookies?

Name _____   Date _____

Stick Puppets

Materials Needed: Popsicle® sticks, glue, paper, cloth, hand-drawn pictures, etc.

Use the section below to draw sketches.

Directions: Reread the literacy part of <u>Lillie Dillie Start Wealthy</u>. Make and name each puppet after a character in the story. After each character is made, retell the section of the story that the characters were in.

Songs

This section has a number of Math Songs followed by some cross-subject songs.

The Multiplication Shake

```
     34
   x 12
     68
 + 340
   408
```

Ah! Multiplication Shake!

Get up! Get up! Yeah!   Multiplication   Shake it! Shake it!

We're going to multiply 34 x 12! Shake! Shake!   Shake! Shake!   Multiplication Shake! Yeah!

Start at the red ones place. Start at the red ones place.
Hop up to the top green multiplicand.

Back it down to the red multiplier.
Slide up and over to the left side.

Back it straight down to the blue tens place.
Slide up and over to the right.

Back it to the left and down to the blue multiplier.
Hop straight up to the top orange multiplicand.

Draw the line and the addition sign.

Add starting from the ones place. Add starting from the ones place. What is your answer?
Those who have 408, have won the race.

You've got it right. Now, shake it to the left.
Shake it right! Shake it up high! Shake it down low! Shake it to the floor.

Now, touch the floor.

Get up and do it again.
You now know more than before.

Enjoy the color-coded multiplication process.
With it, there is no stress.

Let's Get ready! Get Ready!   Get Ready! Do it again! Now, please color-code: 23 x 22.
Did you get 506? If so, you are correct. Now, color-code 33 x 11.   Did you get 363? If so, you are off the chain. Now, color-code 55 x 10. Did you get 550? If so, you're brilliant! Now, color-code 31 x 13.

Ah! Shake it! Shake it! Shake it! Did you get 403? If so, give your neighbor some dap because you are the smartest ever! Now, Shake it to the floor! Shake it to the floor! Shake it to the floor! Shake it to the floor! Multiplication Shake!

Shake it to the left. Shake it to the right. Shake it up high. Shake it down low. Shake it! Shake it! Shake it! Multiplication Shake! Shake it! Multiplication Shake!

Songwriters of "The Multiplication Shake": Leanoria R. Johnson and Ava B. Johnson

I Love D-I- V- I- S- I-O-N!

```
        34
   12 | 408
      - 36↓
        48
      -  48
         0
```

Ah!   D-I- V- I- S- I-O-N   D-I- V- I- S- I-O-N

I love division! I love division! I love division!

Hey! Remember the process.   Do Monkeys Ski?
Divide   Multiply   Subtract
Divide   Multiply   Subtract

Let's divide 408 by 12!   First, ask yourself-   Do I group the first two numbers of my dividend?
Yes or No?   Yes   40!   Remember Do Monkeys Ski?

Divide 40 by 12   and get   You are correct if you got 3.
Now multiply 3 times 12   Get 36   Subtract 36 from 40   Your answer is 4.
Bring down the 8.

48 is your brand dividend.   Then repeat Do Monkeys Ski?

Divide 48 by 12   You are correct if you got 4.
Multiply 4 times 12   You are correct if you got 48.
Now subtract 48 from 48 You should get 0 (zero).

What is your quotient?   Your quotient is 34.   OK! Do four more!

Divide   Multiply   Subtract
Divide   Multiply   Subtract

Divide 209 by 11. Remember to Divide   Multiply   Subtract   You are correct if you got 19.

Now **divide** 400 by 20.   Remember Do Monkeys Ski?   You are correct if you got 20.

Now **divide** 284 by 4.   Work smart! You are correct if you got 71.

Now **divide** 366 by 6. Work it! You are correct if you got 61.

Remember   Divide Multiply   Subtract

D-I-V-I-S-I-O-N   D-I-V-I-S-I-O-N

I love division!   I love division!   I love division!
Hey!   Remember the process.   Do Monkeys Ski?

Divide   Multiply   Subtract
Divide   Multiply   Subtract

Songwriters: Leanoria R. Johnson and Ava B. Johnson

M O N E Y

M O N E Y,   M O N E Y,   M O N E Y

That's what I will   S A V E- O!

I've Got A Budget

I've got a budget. What about you? (repeat 3 times) I'm going up to the top.

I'm on my way. You can, too. (repeat 3 times) I'm going up to the top.

I tell my money what to do. (repeat 3 times) I'm going up to the top.

I spend less than what I earn. (repeat 3 times) I'm going up to the top.

I'll stay on the top. (repeat 3 times) I'm counting on you to come, too.

The Rule of 72 Song

Note: One singer starts out as Jo Jo. The other singers sing the (All) part to Jo Jo. Different students may take turns singing Jo Jo's part.

All: Who put the rule of 72 in the Jo Jo Jar?

All: Jo Jo put the rule of 72 in the Jo Jo Jar.

Jo Jo: Couldn't have been me!

All: Yes, you did!

All: Now, divide 72 by 9.

Jo Jo: How can I?

All: Just divide it! Nine is the interest rate!

Jo Jo: OK. Seventy-two (72) divided by 9 is 8.

Jo Jo: So, it will take 8 years for the money to "double" depending on the economy!

All: Good job, Jo Jo! Yeah! You're a winner!

Place Value Number Sense

Ones, tens, hundreds, drop the comma

Next is thousands!

Ten thousands, hundred-thousands, drop the comma

Next is millions!

Ten millions, hundred millions, drop the comma

Next is billions!

Ten billions, hundred billions, drop the comma

Next is trillions!

Use your number sense!

In the number 7 8 6, 5 4 3, what does the 6 really stand for? What does the 8 really stand for? Try one more! Try one more!

Arms and Angles

Open your arms 90 degrees like a right angle.

Open your arms less than 90 degrees like an acute angle.

Open your arms wider than 90 degrees like an obtuse angle.

Hold them straight out 180 degrees like a straight angle, please!

With ease, make a complete rotation of 360 degrees

Change Percents to Decimals Song

You start with a percent like 66%. You drop the percent sign.

And slide to the left two places.

Place the decimal point in the number like this, 0.66 you see.

When the percent is a single number, like 6%, write a zero (0) before the single number. Again, slide to the left two places.

Place the decimal point in the number like this, 0.06 you see.

The Sides Song

The triangle has 3 sides.

The rectangle has 4 sides

The pentagon has 5 sides.

The hexagon has 6 sides.

The heptagon has 7 sides.

The octagon has 8 sides.

The nonagon has 9 sides.

The decagon has 10 sides.

How many sides do you see when you take your neighborhood ride?

Test Taking Strategies

Get your rest so that you can do your best.

Half of the battle is knowing how to take a test.

Watch out for those extremely frustrating questions.

You have no idea what is the answer, so take an educated guess. Don't waste time.

Before you read a passage, read the stems of the questions.

Circle or jot down the key words. Highlight the key words if you can.

Skim all of the answer choices.

Then go have fun reading the passages being careful to locate key words.

If you are really, really smart, read the passage from the very start.

Paraphrase or reword each sentence and proceed on to win the race.

Win by answering each question at a swift pace.

Reread if you must.

There is only one answer so eliminate the fakes.

Adding Signed Numbers

I'm taking the sign of the larger number!

Is it negative or positive?

Just write the sign. (2x's) Just write it! (2x's)

I'm looking at the two different signs.

I'll subtract the absolute values and get the difference!

Just write the difference. (2x's) Just write it! (2x's)

The middle plus sign is only part of the operation.

That's all it is! Don't mind it! Don't mind it!

I'm taking the sign of the like signs!

Is it negative or positive?

Just write the like sign. (2x's) Just write it! (2x)'s

 I'll add and get the sum!

Just write the sum! (2x's) Just write it! (2x's)

When SUBTRACTING SIGNED NUMBERS –

First, I'll change the sign of the second term.

Second, I'll change the sign of my operation.

Third, I'll follow the addition rules as I did above!   How easy! (2x's)   So easy (2x's)

Samples: (-8) + (+4)= -4   (+9) + (+10) = +19   (-6) + (-6) = -12

(-14) – (-2) = (-14) + (+2) = -12

WRITTEN BY MRS. LEANORIA R. JOHNSON

The Divide Cheer

Give me DIVIDE.

Give me MULTIPLY.

Give me SUBTRACT.

Give me CHECK.

When you work division, first DIVIDE, MULTIPLY, SUBTRACT, until you can't divide any further! Then check!

Or remember- Do Monkeys Ski, CiCi?

Yeah! Yeah! Yeah! Yeah!

The Factors Cheer

Clap 1 X 6.   (Kids clap and say what the leaders say throughout the cheer.)

The product is 6. (kids repeat throughout the cheer)

The factors of 6 are 1 and 6.

Clap 1 X 24.

Clap 2 X 12.

Clap 3 X 8.

Clap 4 X 6.

The product for each one is 24.

The factors of 24 are 1, 2, 3, 4, 6, 8, 12, and 24.

Yeah!!! Yeah!!! Yeah!!! Yeah!!!

Good Hygiene

Get up happily.

Wash your face, brush your teeth.

Take your shower in less than an hour.

Then off to the kitchen to eat.

Eat smart! Think smart! Work smart!

Stay happy and healthy and practice good hygiene.

The Nine Planets

Pluto, what do you know?

I know that I am smallest of them all.

Jupiter, what do you know?

I know that I am the biggest planet.

Mars, what do you know?

I am known as red - O.

 Mercury, what do you know?

I know that I am closest to the Sun.

Venus, what do you know?

I know that I am closest to Earth.

Earth is where I live.

Saturn, what do you know?

I know that I am a giant planet and so are Uranus and Neptune.

C A P I T A L

C (clap hands 4 x's)

A (clap hands 4 x's)

P (clap hands 4 x's)

I (clap hands 4 x's)

T (clap hands 4 x's)

A (clap hands 4 x's)

L (clap hands 4 x's)

That spells CAPITAL!

Use CAPITAL letters with all proper pronouns, I, and all

sentence beginnings!

C (clap hands 4 x's and stomp your feet)

A (clap hands 4 x's and stomp your feet)

P (clap hands 4 x's and stomp your feet)

I (clap hands 4 x's and stomp your feet)

T (clap hands 4 x's and stomp your feet)

A (clap hands 4 x's and stomp your feet)

L (clap hands 4 x's and stomp your feet)

That spells CAPITAL!

Use CAPITAL letters with all proper pronouns, I, and all sentence beginnings!

Other Great Products
by Leanoria R.Johnson, Award-Winning Teacher

Groom To Be Wealthy Workbook

Written for elementary age children through young adults in college, this is a project of triple value. It fills in the financial education gap with hands-on experiences in writing checks, balancing checkbooks, calculating the compound interest and the rule of 72. Transfer life skills learned in the project to real life money management transactions. Work the process for years to build wealth. Maintain and make money work for you.

Math + Money Management = Wealth DVD

A DVD that was created by an award-winning teacher and promises amazement. It is truly amazing to hear insights relating to budgeting and tracking money. All students are influenced to stay the course of building wealth. Live chapter intros and live math dances make this DVD the winner over them all. It's a great training DVD. Use the front cover to teach budgeting principles.

"The Multiplication Shake" Math music CD has a tri-fold value. First, our upbeat CD begins with music that uses dances and colors to teach the processes of multiplication and division. Second, our bonus features are ready-to-print multiplication tables songs, multiplication and division songs that teach strategies to multiply and divide. Third, Five Basic Ways to Solve Word Problems and word problems practice sheets are print-ready! Great music for 5 minute warm up games like "Hot Dog" and "Musical Chairs" on page 58!

Checkbook Register and Other Financial Tracking Tools are proven tools to track real life and real life-like transactions related to checking accounts, savings accounts, debit card, and cash transactions.